Valen

With Values

LIFE
WOULD NOT
BE WORTH
A "CENT"
IF TO BE
MY VALENTINE
YOU'LL NOT
CONSENT

Katherine Kreider

Schiffer Publishing Ltd

77 Lower Valley Road, Atglen, PA 19310

My Dedication

"How do I love thee? Let me count the ways." My dedication is to my "forever valentine" J. David Kreider, my husband and best friend! Thank you for all your love, patience and understanding now and always! Your Queen of Hearts.

Printed in China
ISBN 0-88740-932-6

Published by Schiffer Publishing Ltd.
77 Lower Valley Road
Atglen, PA 19310
Please write for a free catalog.
This book may be purchased from the publisher.
Please include $2.95 for shipping.
Try your bookstore first.

Pop-up garden, once this card is opened this darling Victorian girl hiding in her Secret Garden is revealed, three dimensions, printed in Germany, 3" high, 4" wide, NM, *Kreider Collection*. $5-50

Library of Congress Cataloging-in-Publication Data

Kreider, Katherine.
    Valentines: with values / Katherine Kreider.
      p. cm.
    Includes bibliographical references
    ISBN 0-88740-932-6 (paper)
    1. Valentines--Collectors and collecting--United States--Catalogs.
    I. Title.
NC1866.V3K74 1996
741.6'84--dc20   95-45153
                 CIP

Cover Photo:
Pan's Valentine window display, 24 pieces, Pan Confection Factory, National Candy Co., Inc. Chicago, 1920s.

CONTENTS

Introduction 6

Chapter I   Folk Art Valentines: Handmade 8

Chapter II   The Golden Age: Put Together by Hand 17

Chapter III   Dimensional Valentines 39

Chapter IV   Cultural Valentines: Valentine's Day Lore and

Customs around the World 93

Chapter V   Comic Valentines Through the Ages 100

Chapter VI   Nursery Rhymes and Fairy Tales 120

Chapter VII   Novelty Missives of Love 127

Chapter VIII   Topical Valentines: Flats and Mechanical-Flats 148

Chapter IX   Bits n' Pieces 184

Valentines Manufacturers 188

Glossary 190

Bibliography 192

Moons Mullin with mustache, late 1930s, made in U.S.A., flat, 6" high, 3.5" wide, EX, *Kreider Collection.* $5-55

My Valentine Thank Yous!

A special Valentine Thank You to:

Nancy Rosin from Franklin Lakes, New Jersey, for allowing us into her home to photograph some of her fabulous collection to share with the world!

Julie Barnes, from Omaha, Nebraska, who graciously shared her Black Cherub Fan with the world!

Robert Tholl, coordinator of the "Loveland Re-Mailing Program" in Loveland, Colorado, who generously shared cachets, postmarks and information.

Pamela Schimmel, from Portland, Oregon, who "knew I could do it" and never let me forget it for the last four years!

Marjorie Jackson of Berkley, California, who told me, "You'll make it!" and "Always remember the struggle. As you get older it is the struggles you will remember and miss."

Richard and Beverly Pardini, of Stockton, California, who provided sanctuary to the weary travelers and a haven to pen my book.

Barbara and Jack Wolf. Just think, Mother, if you had never bought me my first three valentines, this book would not have been possible! Thanks Mom! And Thanks Dad for giving Mother the money to pay for the valentines!

Curtis Wolf, my brother. When my camera broke, so did my spirit, but you were there with your Pentex to the rescue! Thanks Little Brother!

"The Susan" and "The Baron" Kessler and Kay for their command of the English language and all of their support over the last six months! Especially to Susan for all of her culinary skills..."see you at 6!"

Anthony Davis, from Universal City, California, for all his verbal support over the last four years.

Jonathan Bulkley, from San Francisco, California, for introducing me to The Ephemera Society of America, Inc.

Please forgive me if I have forgotten anyone. There are many people in the states of California, Oregon, Washington, and Pennsylvania who have been very supportive over the years, from The Oakdale Museum to The California Club in San Francisco. Please consider yourselves each hugged!

This masterpiece is a fine example of "An Era Gone By." "Choked to Death" type valentine, made of celluloid, embellished with satin ribbon and Victorian lady motif hand painted on silk, in original frame with original glass, circa 1870s, frame measures 35" long, 24" wide, 3.5" deep, valentine measures 30" long, 19" wide, *Kreider Collection.*

5

Introduction

What are valentines? Are they collectible? Where do they fit into collections? How much are valentines worth? Who collects valentines? What about valentine reproductions? All of these questions and more will be answered in the pages ahead.

This book gives collectors a guide for pricing items related to Valentine's Day (February 14th) from cards to cachets.

Valentine collectors are a very special group of people, Romantics. We all know what happens to us when we fall in love. The Romantic in us helps to determine the marketplace. One must look at the valentine through the heart and soul of the collector. What might be highly prized by one collector, might not be prized by the next collector. Why?..."**The Heart.**"

There is a significant intangible at play when valentines are bought, sold and collected which is "**The Heart.**" If there were a price equation for buying valentines it would be:

Category + Condition + Size + Manufacturer + Artist signature + Age *Multiplied* by the square root of "**The Heart**" = **A Higher Price.**

As defined, this equation dictates the marketplace.

The value ranges cover poor to near mint condition for each Valentine. Full retail value for mint condition would be off the chart and so is not estimated here. Abbreviations used throughout the book are:

M—Mint: Uncirculated

NM—Near Mint: Was circulated, and usually has a signature written on the back, but there are no creases, pin holes, tears, restoration, etc.

EX—Excellent: The surface of the card has no visible problems, but restoration work could have been done on the back.

VG—Very Good: Creases, fading, pin holes, etc. could appear on this card, along with some restoration work.

P—Poor: Falling apart, torn.

HCPP—Honey Comb Paper Puff

Many collectors of other antiques do not realize that valentines can topically fit into many other collections such as occupational memorabilia, Disney Studios subjects, folk art, or antique advertising, just to name a few. The time has come for valentines to take their rightful place among the world's antique categories. Valentines are not just frivolous missives of love; they also reflect our culture, both past and present. Throughout the ages, valentines have followed themes, from political to fashion. It is our responsibility to preserve these pieces of history for future generations to enjoy.

Finally, please remember that this book was designed to be used. To become worn, soiled and scarred from constant handling would be the best thing that could happen to it and that would give the collector his best reward. With this in mind, let us move on to Chapter 1.

Mary, Mary, quite contrary, flat with easel back, G Trade mark, printed in Germany, 5.5" high, 4" wide, NM, *Kreider Collection.* $5-55

Chapter I
Folk Art Valentines:
Handmade

Some of the earliest valentines were *handmade* dating from the early 1600s. They continue to be made today. Valentines represent many art forms including *Theorem, Fraktur, Scherenschnitte, pin pricking* and *Wycinanki*. Each of these types is prized by collectors of folk art as well as avid valentine collectors.

The *Theorem* style was achieved by sketching an image onto a piece of oiled paper from which a stencil was cut. With the stencil, the image was transferred to another sheet of paper and colored with watercolors. To preserve the painted image, the artist finished the work by brushing gum arabic over the entire image.

In this chapter you will see examples of a Pennsylvania German folk art known as *Scherenschnitte*, pronounced "cher in snit". These are paper pictures carefully cut with scissors. You can still drive over the back roads of Lancaster County, Pennsylvania, in the winter and see this paper cutting art at its best as you peer through the windows of a one-room Amish schoolhouse. Scherenschnitte collages are the most sought after in the world of paper cutting. You can find as many as 100 different colored papers fit into one of these collages. The artist would never think of taking a shortcut by using just one piece of paper. Thousands of images are cut from various colored papers and then very lovingly, but painstakingly, fitted together—as you would piece a jigsaw puzzle—and then secured on a mounting board.

The Pennsylvania German and Swiss were masters of this art form. The Germans took it a few steps further by incorporating *Fraktur* as well as *pin pricking* techniques into their cut work. *Fraktur* can be spelled *Fractur*, either way is acceptable. It is a handwritten script art form (calligraphy) with each letter of the alphabet appearing to be horizontally broken. The Pennsylvania Dutch also used this stylized art form when designing their borders for documents. These decorative borders consisted of birds, angels, hearts, star forms, mermaids, floral patterns, and more. As with other illustrators, the Fraktur practitioner created a distinctive style of sketching and decoration; once it is studied you can learn to identify a particular practitioner's work. During the period circa 1580 through 1750, the Fraktur artists derived their style from many different sources, such as textile pattern books from France, Switzerland, England and Germany.

Love Token/Memorial combination with
original handmade frame composed of
sunflower seeds, buttons, acorn caps, birch
tree pods, dated June 7th, 1889, hair
samples of each child, along with author's
hair braided into a heart, 13" high, 8" wide,
NM, *Kreider Collection.* $50-800

Pin pricking, on the other hand, was achieved by pricking a piece paper
with many different widths of needles and pins to make the most exquisite of
designs. The designs sometimes were hand colored to add a more realistic
touch to the image.

Folk art calligraphic pieces originally were illustrated by clergymen, school-
masters and itinerant artists. They were masters at applying this art form not
only to valentines, but also to marriage and birth certificates, rewards of merit,
and religious and decorative pieces. If you purchase this type of valentine, you
must be very careful to be sure what you are buying since these pieces often
were scripted in German.

Polish peasants also were known for their type of paper cutting called
Wycinanki which was used to represent various events or religious observances.
Their finished work was displayed on windows and walls, just as many people
decorated for each holiday.

Love Token hand cut heart and hair woven into an endless knot, brown and white papers, the name handwritten on the valentine is "Nancy Davis", circa 1825, 3.5" high, 2.75" wide, M, *Rosin Collection.* $25-150

Each of the paper techniques mentioned above is nearly lost today; only a few artisans keep these decorative arts alive. Today, some of the early masterpieces hang in homes of private collectors and in some of the world's leading museums.

Many folk art pieces fit into the category of valentines know as *Love Tokens* which are objects created and given to convey a message from the heart. These tokens are sometimes difficult to distinguish since they can take on many different forms: paperweights, gloves, thimbles, etc. Sailors of yore remembered their sweethearts when out at sea by making tokens of love from seashells or by using their scrimshaw techniques on whales' teeth or anything else they could find.

Among the most sought after love tokens is a series of puzzle valentines known as *rebuses, puzzle purses, acrostics,* or *cryptograms.* All of these puzzles took hours of work and love to create. Puzzle purses were folded-over envelopes with each flap decorated. Usually, the puzzles had a reward placed inside, perhaps a ring or lock of hair. Today's Rubic's cube is reminiscent of yesterday's puzzles; not only are you to open the puzzle correctly, but you also put it back together exactly as it was before.

Other folk art valentines handmade from paper were the watch papers found inside the front and back of a pocket watch. The giver of this love token might have used any of the previously mentioned art forms. These watch papers are prized by valentine collectors, ephemera and watch collectors alike.

Half a Heart valentine, hand watercolored envelope with half of a paper heart inside, 2.75" high, 4.75" wide, circa early 1900s, NM, *Kreider Collection.* $5-75

One of the most important factors for judging old paper ephemera is its condition. I can not stress this enough! The ultimate goal for any collector is to obtain only mint condition specimens, whether they are valentines or any other collectible. This means there is no tolerance for cracks, pin holes, tears, creases, restoration work, etc. *Scherenschnitte, Wycinanki, pin pricking, Theorem,* or *puzzle valentines* are the only forms where creases are acceptable to a discriminating collector. This category of valentine did not have envelopes when it was created. Each valentine would be folded and sealed with wax, then posted by hand and delivered to the sweetheart's doorstep. When the postage rate was established in the United States in 1854, the mail would be prepaid and a postal worker would stamp the envelope with a mark of a dark red circle enclosing a "Paid 5" in the center. To the philatelic collector the envelope is more valuable than the actual valentine.

Watch papers, handmade with hand colored motifs of lovebirds, roses, etc., delicate mementos of love, to keep within one's pocket watch, circa 1800, 2" high, 2" wide, M, *Rosin Collection.* $50-500

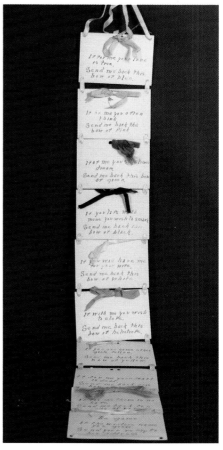

Ribbon valentine: each section has a question and the answer is represented by each ribbon color; therefore, the person picks out the answer and sends the correct color ribbon back, handmade, circa early 1900s. This one is a sad valentine, the ribbon that is missing states: "If for me your heart is dead, send me back this bow of red," 22" high, 8" wide, M, *Kreider Collection.* $15-100

11

Scherenschnitte, of Pennsylvania Dutch
origin, two layers of concentric message
form central design. The remainder of the
all over cut out design includes this
plants and elongated adult-looking cherubs, 20" high, 14" wide, M, *Rosin Collection.* $500-8000

Fractur valentine, Provenance, Virginia,
heart-shaped, with original ribbon laced
throughout its edge, dated 1831, 6" high,
6.5" wide, M, *Rosin Collection.* $500-8000

Scherenschnitte, uncolored, hand cut,
high, 4.5" wide, M, *Rosin Collection.* $
350

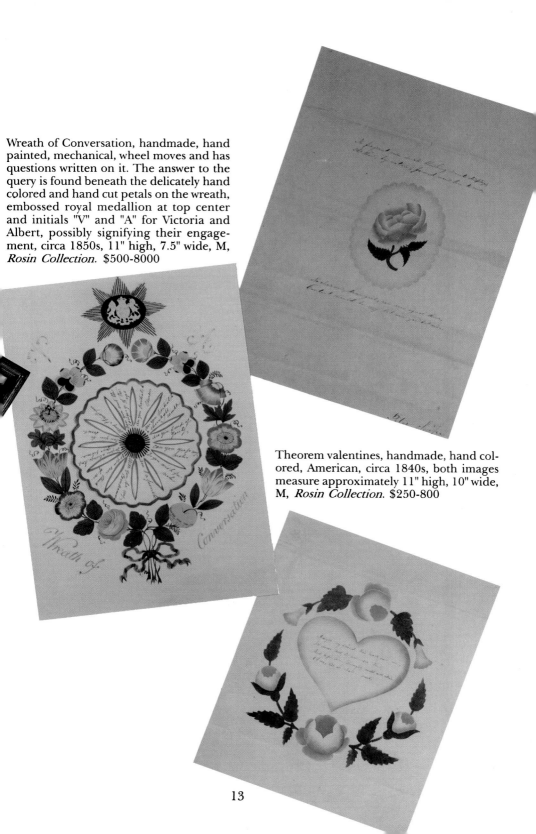

Wreath of Conversation, handmade, hand painted, mechanical, wheel moves and has questions written on it. The answer to the query is found beneath the delicately hand colored and hand cut petals on the wreath, embossed royal medallion at top center and initials "V" and "A" for Victoria and Albert, possibly signifying their engagement, circa 1850s, 11" high, 7.5" wide, M, *Rosin Collection.* $500-8000

Theorem valentines, handmade, hand colored, American, circa 1840s, both images measure approximately 11" high, 10" wide, M, *Rosin Collection.* $250-800

Sailor's valentine, handmade, circa early 1800s. Notice the religious overtones of the anchor, the cross, and the heart, 6.5" high, 4.75" wide, M, *Kreider Collection.* $100-1800

Puzzle Purse valentine, shown closed, M, 4.5" high, 4.5" wide, EX, *Rosin Collection.* This valentine was also featured in *The Valentine Source Book,* published by *The Ephemera Society of America, Inc.* $200-3000

Manuscript valentine, hand colored motif among lithographed gold border with handwritten verse, dated February 14, 1845, 8" high, 5" wide, M, *Kreider Collection.* $25-500

Puzzle Purse valentine, designs of doves and leaves painted with Theorem (stencil) technique. Flower blossoms and hex sign are painted free hand, paper is watermarked 1816, the message would be enclosed within the folds, 12" high, 12" wide, M, *Rosin Collection.* $200-3000

Handmade Native American postcards, with papoose, dated 1908, front of cards, "The Heavenly Twins" and "The Terrible Twins, both from, "Cupid's Square", 4" high, 6" wide, M, *Kreider Collection.* $25-300

A marvelous example of folk art in America. Betty Tuttle was the president of an artist colony in Seattle, Washington, and each holiday the members would hand draw envelopes reflecting imagines of that particular holiday and then usually have them postmarked with an appropriate city relating to that holiday, postmarked Valentine, Nebraska, 6.5" high, 3.75" wide, M, *Kreider Collection.* $5-75

15

"Love's Offering," Victorian scrap valentine in original box, given dimensional appearance utilizing Esther Howland's paper spring innovation, no manufacturers marks, late 1800s. Back of the box with a .3¢ stamp, 5" high, 3" wide, 1/2" deep, EX, *Kreider Collection.*

Chapter II
The Golden Age:
Put Together by Hand

The "Golden Age" of valentines extends from the 1840s to the 1890s when the popularity for Valentine's Day was at its peak. "Put together by hand" valentines made with purchased materials became tremendously popular at that time as well as custom "handmade" valentines. Even today personal "handmade" valentines are still given as tokens of affection.

By the 1840s there were many fine valentine makers and stationers working in Europe. Esther Howland, the First Lady of Valentines, was the first woman ever to make valentines commercially in the United States. Some sources reported that prior to Howland, there were a few New York manufacturers making valentines. Others wrote that she was the first in America and only European makers existed before then. In either case, information to substantiate these claims is lacking.

Howland's business flourished in Worcester, Massachusetts between 1849 and 1880. Her valentines were "put together by hand," not "handmade." She instituted an assembly-line method to construct her cards. One by one, the women workers would piece together each valentine with exquisite embossed paper laces shipped from Europe, hand cut, hand colored, and hand pasted flowers. Once the card reached the last worker, there would be just a few finishing touches and the valentine would be ready to sell.

Miss Howland was responsible for adding some revolutionary changes to the greeting card industry. One was the paper spring, in which small pieces of paper were folded into an accordion style spring and placed under each layer of the valentine card. This method created a new and marvelous effect called the "lift-up" valentine. Another innovative idea was the colored paper wafer placed underneath the coarse paper lace, thereby creating a beautiful softening appearance.

Paper lace makers such as Joseph Mansell, Meek, Dobbs, and Kidd & Co. embossed their names in the lace, usually along the border or sometimes in a more discreet location around the body of the motif. On the other hand, the paper makers would mark the paper with their name and usually a date by using a watermark. The lace makers purchased the watermarked paper to emboss or lithograph and make their own cards. By using both watermarks and embossed marks, one can sometimes identify both the approximate year it was made and the maker of a card. By always keeping a magnifying glass on hand when looking at old valentines, you may be able to see an artist's initials or identifying mark. Keep in mind that watermarks are usually best seen by holding the paper up to strong light.

Velvet covered shadow box valentine with beautiful Victorian lady chromolithographed on the outside, Image 11, inside of box contains a many layered confection embellished with coarse paper lace and Victorian scraps, 1875, 11" long, 8" wide, 4" deep, M, *Rosin Collection.* $100-2000

Not all of Esther Howland's valentines were marked. By studying her marked valentines, you can identify the types of lace she used, the colored wafers she used, and other details. She, as well as other valentine makers in the United States, imported lace, embossed envelopes, and Victorian paper ornaments known as "scraps" from Europe where some of the most important paper lace makers lived and flourished.

Identifying Howland's valentines today is usually possible because she sometimes used one of four distinctive ways to identifying her work:

1.) a small red "H" stamped on the back of the card
2.) a small white heart glued on the back of the card with the red "H" stamped in the middle of the heart
3.) a tiny label with a red "H" stamped in the middle
4.) the initials, N.E.V.Co. imprinted on the card (New England Valentine Company, used during the 1870s.)

Like the young of today who leave the established company to start their own companies, makers of greeting cards in the late 19th century also split from older companies. One which grew into a big valentine manufacturer was George C. Whitney, an ex-employee of Esther Howland. He and his brother Edward Whitney manufactured valentines between 1866 and 1942. Whitney also eventually bought out Esther Howland's business after a near-fatal accident left her father almost helpless in the late 1800s. Whitney's style of making valentines was not much different from Howland's, with the exception that Whitney used a red "W" instead of a red "H" to mark his cards.

The Industrial Revolution took hold of the United States during the 1840s and 1850s and changed the valentine industry forever. Moving away from the delicately handmade and put together by hand valentine cards, valentines were now made with celluloid and coarse paper lace and were bedecked with knots, ribbons and bows. Sometimes referred to as "choked to death," some of these later manufactured valentines can be found in this chapter as well as in the chapter "Novelty Missives of Love."

Valentines made in the mid-1800s in the United States were sold in various price ranges going as high as $50.00 per card. Obviously, only the elite could have afforded cards in that price range. Today, each of the cards previously mentioned could sell for thousands of dollars in the United States and Europe, depending on the buying equation as presented in the Introduction. ("Remember the Heart!")

French soldier and his lady in waiting, greeting card, 1860s, very delicate embossed lace work, lithographed with hand coloring and adorned with Dresden type leaves, 7.75" high, 4.75" wide, EX, *Kreider Collection.* $50-1000

Daguerreotype valentine, late 1800s, fine lace work, adorned with Victorian scrap, put together by hand, 6" high, 4.75" wide, EX, *Rosin Collection.* $75-1000

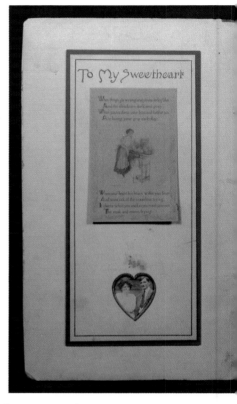

"To My Sweetheart" photograph valentine, flat, 8.5" high, 4.75" wide, VG, *Kreider Collection.* $25-300

"Lovingly Yours", tin type love token, 5.75" high, 3.5" wide, EX, *Kreider Collection.* $25-300

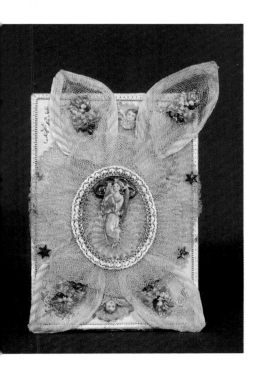

Devotional German memorial, dated 1878, front of the envelope made of gauze fabric and adorned with Victorian scraps with an angel for the center motif. This wood block print was found folded inside the envelope. Also back of envelope. Four folds, envelope measures 4.75" high, 3.75" wide, memorial measures 8.25" high, 5.25" wide, EX. Please note, it may be debatable if devotional cards are considered as valentines. *Kreider Collection.* $50-1000

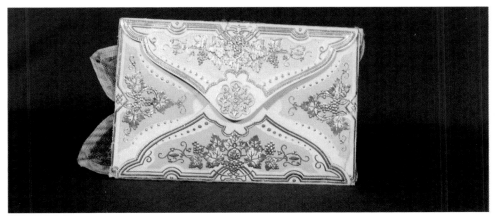

"Endless Knot of Love" copperplate engraving in sepia ink by *Francesco Bartolozzi*, circa 1790, English, watermarked, laid paper, 11.75" high, 8.5" wide, M, *Rosin Collection*. $100-3000

"The Sailor's Farewell," copperplate engraving in sepia ink by *Francesco Bartolo[zzi]*, circa 1790, English, watermarked, laid [pa]per, 11.75" high, 8.5" wide, M, *Rosin [Col]lection*. $100-3000

Victorian lady with Cupid, lithogra[ph] hand colored, adorned with cut out h[and] colored rose, 8" high, 4.75" wide, *Kreider Collection*. $50-500

Wood engraved valentine, hand colored, late 1800s, not the original frame, 9" high, 7.5" wide, EX, *Kreider Collection*. $25-300

Cobweb valentine, lithographed on paper with embossed lace borders, by *Burke,* English, 1840s, central design of flowers evoke messages from "the language of flowers," lifting cobweb's string reveals a delicate hand drawn picture with a message, 10" high, 8" wide, M, *Rosin Collection*. $100-1500

Hand colored litho, accented with "gilding" (brass powder), double page quatro, classical border in corners, circa 1840, 9.75" high, 8" wide, M, *Rosin Collection*. $100-350

23

"Constant," unsigned but attributed to Esther Howland, with hand cut, hand colored and hand pasted scraps, 1848, with original envelope and hand cancelled Ben Franklin .1¢ stamp, 7" high, 4.5" wide, VG, *Kreider Collection.* $100-1000

Attributed to *Esther Howland,* circa 1850, gilt Dresden type basket filled with hand cut, hand colored, and hand pasted bouquet of flowers, adorned with additional gilt Dresden type floral scraps and a cameo embossed ballerina, lace paper makers name is hidden, *Mansell,* 10" high, 8" wide, EX, *Rosin Collection.* $100-500

Civil War era valentine, featuring red, white, and blue ribbons all original, wreath built up from tiny embossed scraps, 7" high, 5" wide, EX, *Rosin Collection.* $25-300

Framed (period framing) quarto, attributed to Esther Howland, circa 1850. Gilt Dresden basket filled with grasses, and mounded into a voluptuous bouquet of heavy, embossed, hand painted flowers. Adorned with additional gilt Dresden floral scraps and a cameo embossed ballerina. Lace paper makers name is hidden, but probably Mansell. Slightly discolored. 11" high, 8.5" wide, EX, *Rosin Collection.* $50-1000

Dresden type gold wreath, delicate lace octavo by Mansell, the central message is printed in silk, 7" high, 4.5" wide, EX, *Rosin Collection.* $25-200

Embossed lace border with hand cut, hand colored and hand pasted flowers, handwritten verse, 11" high, 8.5" wide, NM, *Rosin Collection.* $20-250

Lithographed envelope, front view: the floral enhanced scroll creates a bower for the beloved's name; back view: fine example of this process, 7.5" long, 5" wide, EX, *Rosin Collection.* $5-50

Envelope with example of red sealing wax used to seal envelopes, EX, *Kreider Collection.* $5-30

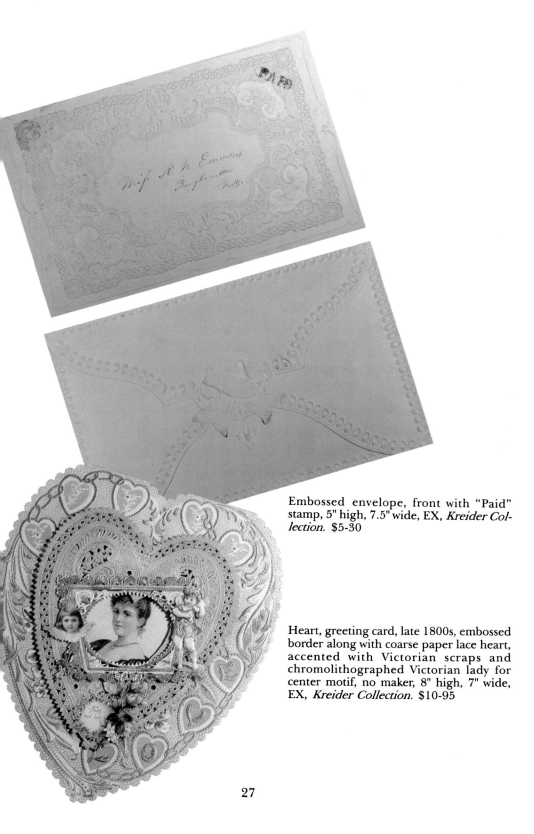

Embossed envelope, front with "Paid" stamp, 5" high, 7.5" wide, EX, *Kreider Collection.* $5-30

Heart, greeting card, late 1800s, embossed border along with coarse paper lace heart, accented with Victorian scraps and chromolithographed Victorian lady for center motif, no maker, 8" high, 7" wide, EX, *Kreider Collection.* $10-95

Unusual combination of monochromatic and chromolithograph center panel, border with coarse paper lace, base of greeting card is embossed, adorned with Victorian scraps, 7.75" high, 5" wide, EX, *Kreider Collection.* $5-75

Chromolithographed and embossed greeting card, late 1800s, accented with silver Dresden type paper lace framing center motif of a sad and lonely girl, 8.5" high, 6.75" wide, EX, *Kreider Collection.* $5-75

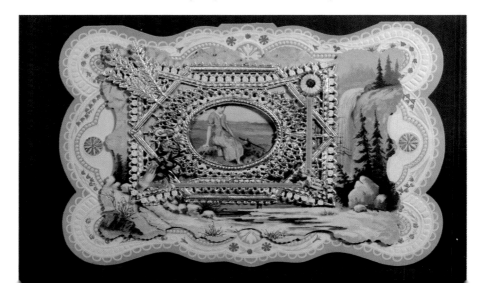

Chromolithograph and embossed greeting
card, late 1800s, each layer has paper
springs behind them to give each layer a
dimensional, coarse paper lace doily is
folded giving an envelope affect, once
opened it reveals the center motif of a beautiful Victorian lady, 10" high, 8" wide, EX,
Kreider Collection. $10-125

Gold foil Dresden type lace border accented with paper wafers of color, framing
chromolitho motif of lady sitting at table,
3.25" high, 4.5" wide, NM, *Kreider Collection.* $5-50

Whitney made valentine, put together by hand using embossed paper lace, Victorian scraps and delicately colored paper wafer giving the lace a softened appearance, dated 1877, writing on the back of the envelope states this card was received when the recipient was two years old, postmarked San Francisco, California, 3.75" high, 3" wide, EX. This valentine was donated by Ken Harrison, Sausolito, California. *Kreider Collection.* $5-75

Art Nouveau artistry exhibited in this greeting card, two layer, chromolitho lady in center, bordered with silver foil paper lace, 8.5" high, 6.5" wide, EX, *Kreider Collection.* $5-95

Embossed, chromolitho greeting card, with bridge over water as center motif, framed by gold foil coarse paper lace, and accented with Victorian scraps, 1880s, 6.75" high, 9" wide, NM, *Kreider Collection.* $5-95

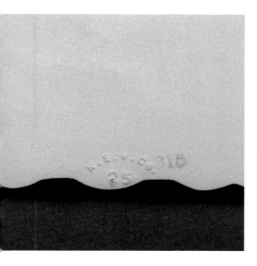

Esther Howlands, greeting card, put together by hand, showing the fine workmanship of one of her many lace makers framing a floral Victorian scrap. The above photo shows the embossed N.E.V. Co. logo, (this stands for New England Valentine Company, during the 1870s), 6" high, 4" wide, NM, *Kreider Collection.* $15-300

glish embossed greeting card, decorated th delicate strips of blue velvet, oval gold l framing, chromolithograph center nel of flowers and Victorian scrap, lace rder is embossed "London" and initials LUMEN," late 1880s, 4.75" high, 3.25" de, NM, *Kreider Collection.* $50-200

Chromolitho die cut greeting card, shaped like urn, cherub as center motif, 1860, 6" high, 6" wide, VG, *Kreider Collection.* $5-75

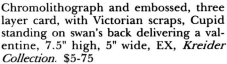

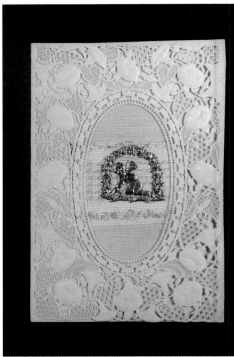

Chromolithograph and embossed, three layer card, with Victorian scraps, Cupid standing on swan's back delivering a valentine, 7.5" high, 5" wide, EX, *Kreider Collection.* $5-75

Morning glory embossed paper lace, with gauze fabric in center panel adorned with gold foil cherub under floral arch, with verse from inside valentine showing through fabric, mid-1800s, 5.5" high, 3.25" wide, NM, *Kreider Collection.* $5-75

Late 1800s, embossed and chromolithograph valentine with Victorian woman as center motif, framed with gold foil paper lace and accented with floral Victorian scraps, 3" high, 4.75" wide, NM, donated by William Frost Mobley, founding father of *The Ephemera Society of America, Inc. Kreider Collection.* $5-75

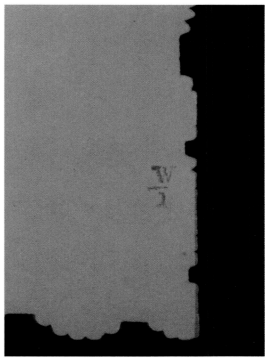

Whitney valentine, embossed, chromolithograph, and Victorian scraps, principal motif is "Cupid's Messengers," two
blue birds, 1880s. Back of card showing
imprinted red "W", 5.5" high, 4" wide, NM,
Kreider Collection. $10-95

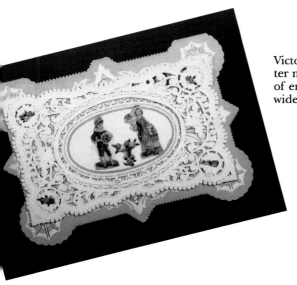

Victorian man and woman scraps as center motif, framed with paper lace over top
of embossed greeting card, 3" high, 4.25"
wide, EX, *Kreider Collection.* $5-75

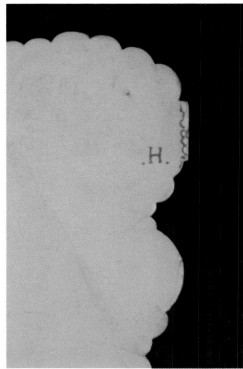

"To One I Love," embossed, chromolithograph, center motif with arrow through signed message framed with silver foil paper lace and accented with hearts of fire Victorian scraps, seen quit often on devotional cards. Gold initial "H" on back of card, 7.75" high, 5" wide, EX, *Kreider Collection.* $5-125

Shadow box valentine, in original frame, put together by hand, made of Dresden type gold foil butterflies, parchment, embossed paper lace accented with silk with chromolithographed heart-shaped spider web as principal motif, made in Germany, mid-1800s, 13" high, 11.5" wide, valentine only, shadow box 15" high, 15" wide, 3" deep, M. Donated by Thomas Watling, Jr., Turlock, California. *Kreider Collection.* $25-1800

"A Gift of Love" valentine, chromolithograph, embossed motif of a darling Victorian child in square insert of bamboo with ladybug crawling up one of the bamboo shoots, flat with easel back, bordered with burgundy velvet, initials O.B., 10.5" high, 8.5" wide, EX, *Kreider Collection.* $5-125

"Choked To Death" hanging valentine, principal motif is made of celluloid hand painted with a basket of roses and "Love's Greetings," in original box lined with coarse paper lace, adorned with ribbons, bows and knots, 1909. Valentine only 7.5" high, 9.25" wide; box 8" high, 10" wide, 1.25" deep, NM, *Kreider Collection.* $35-1200

Envelope type valentine made of celluloid, satin, hand painted on silk, border with satin cord. Chantilly lace and frame were added later, 13.5" high, 10.5" wide, valentine only, M, *Kreider Collection.* $25-500

"Choked To Death" greeting card, elaborate lace confection, unsigned, *Esther Howland*, lace by *Mansell,* multiple layering and add-ons include chenille, embossed flowers and gilded ribbon, circa 1850s, 9.5" high, 8" wide, NM, *Rosin Collection.* $25-500

All valentines are Whitney put-together-by-hand greeting cards, circa 1920s, embossed and chromolithograph, accented with scraps and paper springs originally invented by Esther Howland. All are imprinted on the back "Whitney Made, Worcester Mass." Measurements 4 to 8" high, 4 to 6" wide, all EX, *Kreider Collection.* $5-50

Chapter III
Dimensional Valentines

Dimensional valentines are defined by their length, width, height, and depth, along with the number of layers on each card. They date from the late 1800s to the 1930s. In the past these cards were virtually forgotten and have been placed into the ephemeral category. Some people refer to this type of card as "three dimensional" or from time to time, "mechanical." These terminologies are incorrect. Each card can have many dimensions, the true mechanical valentine has one or more moving parts. The parts on a dimensional card pull out or pop up. The are *not* controlled by a series of mechanical pulls or tabs like you find on a mechanical card.

The lithography process played a very important part in the production of valentines from the 1840s to around the 1860s. With the refinement of this printing process and the demand for more valentines, the job description of artist/illustrator became quite important. The artist/illustrator would draw an image directly onto the stone used in the lithography process. These stones were made of a very heavy limestone, from three to six inches high and perfectly flat. Once the printer achieves the number of cards they want to print, they can then grind or resurface these stones and continue to make many more cards from that same stone. Most of these stones were destroyed over the years. If you are lucky enough to run across one of them today, you will have a very rare piece to add to your collection.

It is important to realize that in lithography only one color was used (usually black or brown) and only one stone was used. As you look through the other chapters in this book, you will see fine examples of this. Once printed, each valentine would be hand colored. As time progressed, a new and improved process was added, *chromolithography*. You could now print with many colors by using one stone per color.

As you start to examine lithograph, valentines with verses imprinted in the center, you begin to wonder how in the world they were ever made. Not only did the artist/illustrator have to know how to sketch in reverse, they also had to hand write the message in reverse. Imagine writing and drawing in reverse! It would be very difficult to reproduce valentines of this quality today and prices per card would be astronomical. Once you study the dimensional cards throughout this chapter and the valentines in the other chapters, you will see that chromolithography is truly an art form representing the best American and European printers of the past.

Victorian girl standing on top of a four leaf clover being held by Cupid, chromolitho die cut, no maker, dimensional, 10" high, 7" wide, 5" deep, NM, *Kreider Collection.* $20-275

There are many important artists who have contributed to the world of valentine illustrations throughout the decades. Unfortunately, they did not always sign their work. As you study the various artists designs, you will start to recognize an artist's work even when it is not signed. Francis Brundage and Grace Wiederseim Drayton both worked for Raphael Tuck and Sons. Grace Drayton is the originator of the Campbell kids (for Campbell Soup Co. Advertising). Her period of illustrating for Tuck was a short one, therefore her cards signed or unsigned are considered to be a valuable asset to a collection. Francis Brundage started working for Tuck around 1903 and died in 1937. She is best known for her illustrations of Victorian, Black, and Dutch children, and her unique style of drawing Black adults. Francis would weave her initials "FB" together and discreetly place them somewhere on the original drawing. This is indicative of many artists then and now. It is not uncommon to find initials or a signature intertwined into an illustration where you would least expect to find one.

"To My Sweetheart" tri-motor airplane, dimensional, with original crepe paper wings, filled with three little girls flying to their Sweethearts, top of airplane made of HCPP, printed in Germany, circa 1930s, 6" high, 14" long, 4" deep, EX, *Kreider Collection.* $20-350

Raphael Tuck and Sons were in business from 1866 with offices in London and New York. Their high standards could never be surpassed. They used only the best materials in their cards including the finest inks. Tuck was also a genius when it came to marketing his cards. He had competitions to get the public to buy more cards, much like the Hallmark company does today with their Gold Crown Card club. Tuck's logo is one you need to remember as you study valentines. In 1881 they implemented their new trademark of the palette and easel, as will be seen in the chapter "Missives of Love."

Three dimensional valentine with bi-wing airplane as the center motif, accented with Victorian child and flowers, dated February 14, 1930, printed in Germany, 9.5" high, 6" wide, 3" deep, NM, *Kreider Collection.* $20-225

Included in the dimensional category are valentines made with honey comb paper puff, abbreviated HCPP. HCPP is tissue paper folded and glued into an accordion style imitating a honey bee's comb. One of the primary manufacturers of honey comb paper puff cards was The Beistle Co. of Shippensburg, Pennsylvania. HCPP cards enjoyed their greatest popularity in the 1920s in the United States. Originally, these cards could be purchased for from .5¢ to .25¢ a card; today they can be priced from $10.00 to several hundred dollars. Many of this type are pulled open and secured with a small metal tab to give the valentine its dimensional appearance. Another variety of HCPP has an easel back with a cloth or folded piece of paper which falls over the easel to keep the card from closing. HCPP also was used as an embellishment on many dimensional cards. They came in a variety of colors including vivid red. Many colors were air brushed onto the cards. One of the most widely used colors was dusty peach. Many times, people will ask "was this originally a vivid red?" But the answer is no. When fading occurs on a card, it never happens evenly. If you take a look into the center of the honeycomb part, you will see that the dusty peach is consistent throughout—and therefore has not faded.

About twenty years ago, you could purchase a dimensional card between $1 and $50. Today, the same card, depending on condition, category, manufacturer, and whether it was signed by the artist or not, could command from several hundred to a thousand dollars. It is important to keep in mind that as a collections are unveiled, this will flood the marketplace with new material, creating a fluctuation in prices. Again, please remember the buying equation described in the Introduction.

Airplane hanging on original string giving this card a mechanical affect, Germany, 6" high, 5" wide, .5" deep, NM, *Kreider Collection*. $15-75

Dimensional airplane flying over what appears to be an illustration of an exhibition building, artist Ernest Nister, London, printed in Bavaria, manufactured by, E.P. Dutton & Co., New York, #2783, with easel back, 4.5" high, 4" wide, 4" deep, NM, *Kreider Collection.* $25-125

"Just A Plane Valentine," single engine dimensional airplane, with mechanical prop, accented with HCPP and young couple flying high, 6" high, 10.75" long, 7.5" wide, 1.5" deep, this airplane also comes in green, yellow and blue, printed in Germany, *Kreider Collection.* $25-350

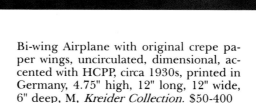

Bi-wing Airplane with original crepe paper wings, uncirculated, dimensional, accented with HCPP, circa 1930s, printed in Germany, 4.75" high, 12" long, 12" wide, 6" deep, M, *Kreider Collection.* $50-400

Single engine airplane, embellished with
Victorian scraps, and two Victorian children in cockpit, printed in Germany, 6.5"
high, 13" long, 3" deep, 14" wide, NM,
Kreider Collection. $35-350

Steam and sail combination, three dimensional, accented with Victorian scraps,
sailor boy on deck, with original cellophane
in the portholes, some restoration, 9.75"
high, 11.5" wide, 3.75" deep, VG, *Kreider
Collection.* This valentine is a particular
favorite among collectors and can be usually found in a collection. $35-500

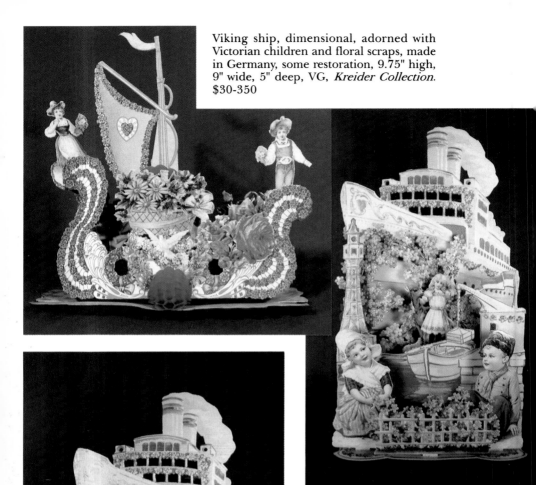

Viking ship, dimensional, adorned with Victorian children and floral scraps, made in Germany, some restoration, 9.75" high, 9" wide, 5" deep, VG, *Kreider Collection*. $30-350

Steamships with four dimensions, with original cellophane in windows, both printed in Germany, both 10.5" high, 6" wide, 3.5" deep, NM, *Kreider Collection*. These two steamships are perfect examples of why the completion of a valentine collection is nearly impossible. Many times the primary piece of the valentine would be used over and over again; the center motifs here are entirely different. One is a Victorian girl with a fawn and the other is a Victorian boy with a dog. $35-350

46

Blue sailboat with sailor child, roses and HCPP, three dimensions, printed in Germany, 9" high, 7.5" wide, 3" deep, EX, *Kreider Collection.* $20-175

"Red Sails in the Sunset," sails made of HCPP, two dimensions, sailboat is adorned with Victorian children and swans on the deep blue sea, 11.75" high, 9.5" wide, 4.25" deep, VG, *Kreider Collection.* This valentine originally sold for .25¢. $30-325

Pink sailboat with forget-me-nots, roses, lilies of the valley, with HCPP, dated February 14th, 1930, printed in Germany, 12" high, 11" wide, 3.5" deep, EX, *Kreider Collection.* Note: this ship is exactly the same imagine as the previous valentine with two distinctive differences, size and color. $30-325

Sailboat with sailor boy, airbrushed HCPP base, 9.5" high, 8" wide, 2.5" deep, Germany, NM, *Kreider Collection.* $25-225

Uncirculated, three dimensional ship and sailboat combination, printed in Germany, 1930s, 9.5" high, 5.5" wide, 2.75" deep, M, *Kreider Collection.* $30-300

Airplane with lobster hanging off the wind, mechanical, dimensional, with easel back, uncirculated, printed in Germany, 1930s, 10.5" high, 8.75" wide, 9" deep, M, *Kreider Collection.* $15-175

Steam Locomotive, three dimensions with Victorian children and lots of roses, circa 1915, some restoration, 7" high, 8" wide, 5" deep, VG, *Kreider Collection.* $25-250

Steam locomotive, three dimensions with a Victorian boy and girl, 1909, 6" high, 7" wide, 2.5" deep, VG, *Kreider Collection.* $20-200

Fancy steam locomotive by Ambassador Cards, sold for .75¢ in the early 1960s, very unusual motif for a Mother's valentine card, 7.5" high, 9.5" wide, 5" deep, NM, *Kreider Collection.* $5-50

Pink locomotive with 4-4 wheel configuration, dimensional, body made of HCPP, with original cellophane windows and lights, accented with pink roses, unmarked, circa 1930s, also comes in blue, 7" high, 8" wide, 5" deep, EX, *Kreider Collection.* $30-325

Blue forget-me-not steam locomotive filled with lilies of the valley and two charming angels looking on, Germany, 4.5" high, 5" wide, 1" deep, *Kreider Collection.* $5-50

Observation car, chromolithograph, manufactured by Raphael Tuck & Sons. Back of
car opens up to add a wonderful three dimensional affect of dove cotes, doves, and
flowers, 8.5" high, 5.5" wide, 3" deep, EX,
Kreider Collection. $30-300

"Valentine Limited Lovers Line" rear of
observation car, deck filled with Campbell
soup-type children and a black porter,
made in U.S.A., 6" high, 5" wide, 1.5" deep,
EX, *Kreider Collection* This valentine
would fit into the collections of train collectors as well as black memorabilia collectors. $10-125

Double donkeys pulling chariot with blue forget-me-nots, lilies of the valley and identical twin girls, printed in Germany, 7" high, 9" wide, 6.75" deep, NM, *Kreider Collection*. $35-325

Shetland pony pulling wagon, wheels are mechanical, dimensional, made in U.S.A., 8" high, 10" wide, 2" deep, VG, *Kreider Collection*. $10-150

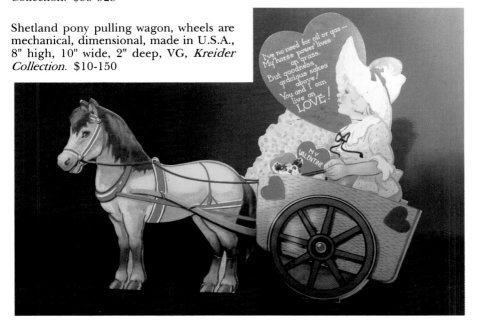

Shetland pony pulling cart, wheels are mechanical, dimensional, made in Germany, no maker, 1920s, 7" high, 11" wide, 2" deep, VG, *Kreider Collection.* $10-150

Rickshaw carrying darling little girl to her valentine, pulled by two white turtle doves, top of rickshaw is made of HCPP, printed Germany, no maker, also comes in blue, 8.5" high, 7.5" long, 6" deep, EX, *Kreider Collection.* $25-275

Horse drawn Victoria driven by Victorian boy, made by Raphael Tuck & Sons, early 1900s, embellished with forget-me-nots, original reins still intact, 7" high, 10.5" wide, 5" deep, *Kreider Collection.* $35-400

Carriage pulled by two white turtle doves, carrying a young lady with her ukulele and flowers, mechanical, printed in Germany, 7" high, 9.5" long, 2.5" deep, EX, *Kreider Collection.* $25-275

Leaf carriage, filled with children and roses, wheels made of forget-me-nots, accent of HCPP, printed in Germany, 6.5" high, 10.75" long, 3.25" deep, EX, *Kreider Collection.* $25-275

Rose covered carriage pulled by two swallows, four silver foil wheels, printed in Germany, 8" high, 10" wide, 5.5" deep, EX, *Kreider Collection.* $25-275

Three-wheeled carriage driven by cherub and two white turtle doves, accented with forget-me-nots and roses, with a HCPP heart motif, some restoration, printed in Germany, 9.5" high, 9.5" wide, 2.5" deep, EX, *Kreider Collection.* $30-325

Magnificent example of a five-dimensional Gondola, embellished with lots of Victorian scraps and still has original string on the end of the fishing pole, accented across the front with HCPP, printed in Germany, no maker, 10" high, 12" wide, 4.5" deep, NM, *Kreider Collection.* $50-500

Gondola manufactured by Raphael Tuck & Sons, with original cellophane in lanterns, Victorian scraps and HCPP, circa early 1900s, printed in Germany, 7" high, 10.5" long, 5" deep, EX, *Kreider Collection.* $35-400

Gondola, uncirculated, on wheels and adorned with Victorian scraps, printed in Germany, 10.5" high, 10.5" long, 4.5" deep, M, *Kreider Collection.* $35-375

On the waters of Venice guided by Cupid taking his lovely Psyche where he can keep her out of harm's way, dimensional, chromolithograph, canopy made of HCPP, 6.5" high, 15" long, 2.5" deep, VG, *Kreider Collection.* $25-300

Rowboat filled with hearts, cherubs and kitten, dimensional, with easel back, Germany, 5" high, 6" long, 1.5" deep, NM, *Kreider Collection.* $10-75

1940s wooden speed boat, unsigned but attributed to Charles Twelvetrees, top of boat made of HCPP therefore giving the boat a dimensional look, no maker, made in U.S.A., 10.5" high, 10" long, 2" deep, EX, *Kreider Collection.* $5-50

Dirigible and car combination, two dimensions, 1930s, made in Germany, 9" high, 7" long, 1" deep, EX, *Kreider Collection.* $10-175

Hot air balloon, four dimensions, filled with Victorian rose scraps and Cupid, printed in Germany, 9.5" high, 6" wide, 2.75" deep, EX, *Kreider Collection.* $35-350

Four-door convertible with house in the background, three dimensional, 1915, adorned with HCPPs and Victorian scraps, printed in Germany, 10.5" high, 11" long, 4" deep, X, *Kreider Collection.* $35-400

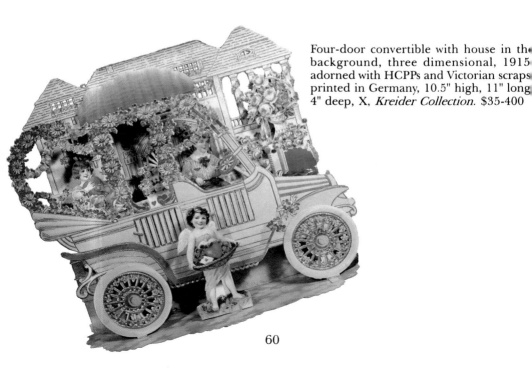

Four-door touring sedan with children riding inside, with original HCPP for the hood and cellophane for the windows, early 1930s, printed in Germany, 7" high, 12" long, 5" deep, NM, *Kreider Collection.* $35-400

Roadster with jump seat in back, uncirculated, dimensional, adorned with blue forget-me-nots, roof made of HCPP, spoked wheels, printed in Germany, 8" high, 11.5" long, 3" deep, M, *Kreider Collection.* $35-400

Four-door sedan with open driver cab, 1920s, dimensional, driven by Cupid carrying children onward to Valentine's Day, 1920s, spoked wheels, 6.5" high, 11.75" long, 2" deep, EX, *Kreider Collection.* $30-375

Hallmark single-seat convertible driven by a cherub, two dimensions, sold for $1.00, early 1960s. One has a pink car while the other has a blue car, possible series, 8.5" high, 6.5" long, 4" deep, NM, *Kreider Collection.* $5-50

"Love's Auto" two-seated roadster with
hand crank, early 1900s, one dimensional
with easel back, 5" high, 10" long, NM,
Kreider Collection. $25-275

Darling child dressed in her winter attire,
carrying Chinese chrysanthemums and
pulling a wagon full of hearts and cherub,
with original ribbon, dimensional, 8.5"
high, 4.75" long, 2.5" deep, *Kreider Collection.* $15-125

"Car Loads of Affection," pastel blue, the only difference from the previous valentine is that on this car the HCPP is not scalloped, NM, *Kreider Collection.* $20-225

Double pastel blue swan carriage, with wheels, HCPP, dimensional, children inside, 8.5" high, 10.75" long, 3" deep, NM, *Kreider Collection.* $20-225

Double pastel pink horses pulling rickshaw with children inside, 8.25" high, 11" long, 3" deep, NM, *Kreider Collection* Possible series with other images. $20-225

"Car Loads of Affection," pastel pink four-door sedan, late 1930s, the roof is made of scalloped HCPP, no manufacturer's marks, 8.5" high, 11.75" long, 3" deep, NM, *Kreider Collection.* $20-225

Three-dimensional valentine with angel setting hearts afire, adorned with white turtle dove and original cellophane in window, printed in Germany, 8.5" high, 6" wide, 2" deep, EX, *Kreider Collection.* $20-200

Child on swing surrounded by a four-leaf clover and forget-me-nots, four dimensions, made in Germany, 8.75" high, 6" wide, 3.5" deep, EX, *Kreider Collection.* $25-200

The Secret Garden, complete with trellises, fountain, flowers and children, exceptional piece, uncirculated, printed in Germany, 10" high, 13" wide, 4" deep, M, *Kreider Collection.* $35-400

Cherub peering out from two vases of daffodils holding two hearts with original satin ribbon, circa early 1900s, Germany, 6.25" high, 4" wide, .75" deep, EX, *Kreider Collection.* $15-95

Cupid kneeling on daisy getting ready to shoot the arrow of love into an unexpecting heart, holding two hearts with original ribbon, with easel back. Envelope on Daisy opens up to reveal "Love's Offering" 6.5" high, 5" wide, 3" deep, M, *Kreider Collection.* $10-125

upid is busy reading a note from his true ve Psyche, lampshade made of HCPP, imensional, no maker, 8.75" high, 4.5" ide, 3" deep, EX, *Kreider Collection.* $10-25

Cupid sharpening one of his arrows before he sets out to make another heart fall in love, dimensional, 4.75" high, 4" wide, 2.5" deep, NM, *Rosin Collection.* $10-125

Cupid building a brick wall around his heart, three dimensions, chromolithograph, Germany, 8" high, 6" wide, 3.75" deep, NM, *Kreider Collection.* $10-125

Dutch boy and girl carrying crock of three dimensional tulips, chromolithograph, with easel back, sold for .10¢, manufactured by Raphael Tuck & Sons, printed in Germany, 8" high, 6" wide, crock is 1" deep, EX, From The *Kreider Collection.* $20-175

Cupid on his way to deliver his hearts in a chariot of lilacs, artist-signed by Ellen Clapsaddle, 5.5" high, 6" wide, 3.5" deep, EX, *Kreider Collection.* $15-150

This little baby doll is wishing you a happy valentines day, possible unsigned artist, Germany, 6.5" high, 4" wide, 2" deep, EX. Note how the primary piece was used in these two images, only the center motif was changed, *Kreider Collection.* $15-125

This wondering little boy wants to know if you will be his valentine, three dimensional, accented with violets, HCPP and roses, underside of valentine states: "There is a Heart to suit you aye, One that will faithful to you stay, Need I tell you that Heart is mine, will you then by my valentine. [sic]" Germany 6.5" high, 4" wide, 2" deep, EX, *Kreider Collection.* $15-125

Black messenger holding box of three dimensional flowers, with easel back, chromolithograph die cut, early 1900s, 9.5" high, 5" wide, box is 2" deep, NM, box shown open, manufactured by Raphael Tuck & Sons, printed in Germany, *Kreider Collection.* $25-250

Matching postcard to previous valentine, Tuck's valentine series #107, 1906, 5.5" high, 3.5" wide, EX, *Kreider Collection.* $5-50

...place with cat attached with original ...n ribbon, chromolithograph die cut, ...le in Germany, possible series for im-...s; would also fit well into a tennis or a ...collector's collection. One measures, ... high, 5.5" wide, 1" deep; other mea-...s, 7" high, 6" wide, 1" deep, EX, both *...ider Collection.* $15-125

Collie attached to his dog house with original chain, made in Germany, 6.75" high, 6" wide, 1.5" deep, EX, possible series. *Kreider Collection.* $15-125

Fabulous St. Bernard dog attached with original metal chain to his dog house, two dimensional chromolithograph die cut, some restoration, Germany, 10" high, 10" wide, 2" deep, EX. There is also a smaller version of this valentine. This valentine would be of particular interest to the collector of pure bred dogs. Many valentines use generic-looking dogs, so when you find one with a pure bred, you have found a winner. *Kreider Collection.* $35-350

Unusual dimensional and mechanical valentine with Bull Mastif and kitten eating their evening meal, along with a lady dressed in a valentine costume, 8.5" high, 8" wide, 2 deep, EX, *Kreider Collection.* $15-125

Victorian child holding baby doll and turtle dove on original string among the lilies of the valley, forget-me-nots and roses, printed in Germany, 9" high, 4.75" wide, 3.5" deep, EX, *Kreider Collection.* $25-250

Victorian child holding baby doll with dove cote in the background, accented with roses, four dimensions. Another valentine also used the same little girl with her doll as the principal motif, 9.5" high, 6.5" wide, 2.75" deep, NM. This card would also appeal to doll collectors. *Kreider Collection.* $25-250

Victorian boy reading book, three dimensional chromolithograph, embellished with roses, lilacs and forget-me-nots, printed in Germany, 9.5" high, 7" wide, 2.75" deep, NM. This valentine would appeal to librarians as well as antiquarian book dealers, *Kreider Collection.* $25-250

Another version of a dove cote filled with doves, accented with Victorian scraps of children and vases with daffodils and forget-me-nots, roof over dove cote made of HCPP, early 1900s, Germany, 8.5" high, 4.75" wide, 3.5" deep, EX, *Kreider Collection.* $20-225

Exquisite dove cote made of HCPP, four dimensions, adorned with chromolithographed Victorian die cut scraps of roses and children, no maker, 13" high, 10" wide, 3.75" deep, EX, *Kreider Collection.* $35-375

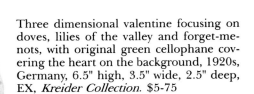

Three dimensional valentine focusing on doves, lilies of the valley and forget-me-nots, with original green cellophane covering the heart on the background, 1920s, Germany, 6.5" high, 3.5" wide, 2.5" deep, EX, *Kreider Collection.* $5-75

"Hold To Light" Victorian log cabin, four dimensions, uncirculated, embellished with all sorts of Victorian scraps and HCPP, 1900-1920s, printed in Germany, 10" high, 9.5" wide, 4.5" deep, M, *Kreider Collection.* $35-400

"Hold To Light" two dimensional with darling Victorian girl surrounded with pink forget-me-nots, 1925, Germany, 8.5" high, 6" wide, 3" deep, NM, *Kreider Collection.* $25-250

"Hold To Light" fountain with base of fountain made of HCPP, with easel back, uncirculated, printed in Germany, 11" high, 8" wide, 3" deep, M, *Kreider Collection.* $30-350

Rose motif three dimensional accented with HCPP, circa 1920s, printed in Germany, 9.75" high, 7" wide, 4.5" deep, EX, *Kreider Collection.* $25-250

Cupid fine and tall bringing his true love, Psyche, this wonderful bouquet of flowers, three dimensions, adorned with HCPP arches and Victorian scraps, Germany, 11" high, 6.5" wide, 4.25" deep, EX, *Kreider Collection.* $25-250

Victorian porch with white picket fence, trellis and Victorian children bringing valentines to one another, HCPP accents, early 1900s, printed in Germany, 10" high, 9.5" wide, 4.25" deep, VG, *Kreider Collection.* $50-400

Victorian ladies blowing heart-shaped bubbles, three dimensions, chromolithograph, no maker, 10" high, 7" wide, 3.75" deep, EX, *Kreider Collection.* $25-275

Harp, die cut, with Victorian children bringing flowers to their loved ones, no maker, 1914, 4.75" high, 2.5" wide, 1.75" deep, VG, *Kreider Collection.* $5-35

Harp, die cut, accented with Victorian scraps and HCPP base, printed in Germany, 8" high, 4" wide, 2.5" deep, EX, *Kreider Collection.* From harps to banjos, instrument collectors are always looking for a fabulous image to add to their collections. $15-125

Harp with parchment paper that folds out to give a dimensional appearance, morning glories and hearts with child adorn the strings of the harp, with easel back, 7.25" high, 5.5" wide, EX, *Kreider Collection.* $10-95

Phonograph with angels handing out hearts to a precious Victorian school girl, circa 1920s. Notice the needle of the phonograph is still intact, 6.75" high, 11" long, 3.5" deep, EX, *Kreider Collection.* $30-325

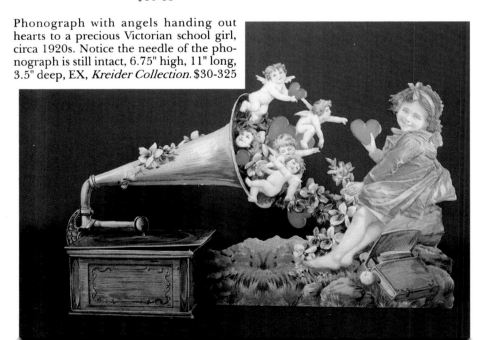

Big-eyed couple dancing the night away as the moon rises, images of the phonograph, child directing, and moon are in the background, chromolithograph die cut with great color, 1920s. The most important aspect of this valentine is the boy smoking. It is difficult to find valentines showing smoking paraphernalia. 12" high, 11" wide, 5.5" deep, EX, *Kreider Collection.* $25-250

Cupid playing the baby grand piano while children are dancing, 9" high, 11" wide, NM, *Rosin Collection.* $25-275

Cupid playing "My Funny Little Valentine," dimensional, Germany, missing rail accent on top of organ, 9.5" high, 8.75" wide, 6" deep, VG, *Kreider Collection.* $25-275

Heart made of parchment, dimensiona
affect, chromolithograph heart as center
motif with cherub, easel back, early 1900s
7" high, 6.5" wide, NM, *Kreider Collection*
$10-95

Open-up hearts with four dimensional
scenes inside: hearts closed and opened
both are filled with Victorian scraps of children, flowers and birds, printed in Germany, both measure 4.5" high, 4" wide, 4.5"
deep, NM, *Kreider Collection.* $10-95

Open-up heart with three-dimensional scene inside, heart closed and heart opened revealing a mother, her child and dog made of chromolithographed die cut scraps, 3.5" high, 3.5" wide, 3.5" deep, NM, *Kreider Collection*. $5-75

Flower garden with Victorian little boy pushing Dresden type gold wheelbarrow filled with daisies, made in Germany, 4" high, 8" wide, 5.5" deep, EX, *Kreider Collection*. $10-95

Hot air balloon made of HCPP airbrushed with Victorian ladies sitting on the edge of the basket, circa early 1900s, Germany, some restoration, 11.75" high, 9" wide, 5" deep, EX, *Kreider Collection.* $30-375

Honeycomb paper puff pedestal with angels delivering love letters, made in U.S.A., dimensional, 10.5" high, 9" wide, 4" deep, EX, *Kreider Collection.* $10-125

82

ushroom made of HCPP with Victorian
ldren and forget-me-nots, Germany,
.75" high, 9" wide, 5" deep, EX, *Kreider
llection.* $25-250

neycomb paper puff pedestal with an-
delivering hearts, double HCPP base,
de in U.S.A., dimensional, 10.5" high,
' wide, 4.25" deep, EX, *Kreider Collec-
1.* Note: these valentines are not faded,
is their original color. $10-125

83

Big-eyed children kissing in a rose bush with a California snail and puppy looking on, base made of HCPP, circa 1920s, printed in Germany, 9.5" high, 9" wide, 3" deep, EX, *Kreider Collection.* $20-200

Perfume atomizer with big-eyed children, base of bottle made of HCPP, top of atomizer is given definition with HCPP, has original envelope with .2¢ Canadian stamp, circa 1920s, 8.75" high, 6.5" wide, 2.5" deep, NM, *Kreider Collection.* $25-250

Big-eyed child hiding behind arm chair while another is reading a book and two cats are eating. The other has a stage coach pulled by a snail and driven by a big-eyed child, both images made in Germany, the first 3.5" high, 2.75" wide, .5" deep; the other 3.5" high, 2.75" wide, .5" deep, both images EX, *Kreider Collection.* $3-35

Whimsical big-eyed court jester serenades big-eyed couple with their pets, printed in Germany, dimensional, 9.5" high, 9" wide, 1.75" deep, EX, *Kreider Collection.* $20-225

Cowgirl with pony as center motif along with Campbell Soup kid images, three dimensional, unsigned but attributed to Grace Drayton, 9.5" high, 8" wide, 3" deep, EX, *Kreider Collection.* $25-250

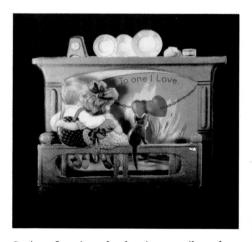

Series of unsigned valentines attributed to Grace Drayton, all printed in Germany. The number in the series is unknown at this time, all measure approximately, 3.5" high, 3.5" wide, 1" deep, EX, *Kreider Collection.* $5-50

Grandfather clock surrounded with images of key, arrow, hearts and horseshoe, three dimensional, uncirculated, printed in Germany, 10" high, 6.5" wide, 3" deep, M, *Kreider Collection.* $20-225

Cherub with golden wheelbarrow of roses and quilted heart for background motif, three dimensional, made by Hallmark and sold for $2.00, 9.5" high, 7" wide, 4.5" deep, NM, *Kreider Collection.* $5-50

Wishing well in the middle of a grove of trees, two dimensions, early 1960s, made by Hallmark, 9.5" high, 7" wide, 4.5" deep, NM, *Kreider Collection.* $5-35

Cinderella type castle, three dimensional, dusted with silver sparkles, 1958, made by Hallmark, sold for $1.00, 9.5" high, 15" wide, 4.75" deep, NM, *Kreider Collection.* $10-125

Cinderella coach to go with the Hallmark castle, made by Hallmark, three dimensions, 9.75" high, 7.5" wide, 4.5" deep, EX, *Kreider Collection*. $1-35

Valentine fairies come in this carriage to bring you valentine wishes, three dimensional, late 1950s, made by Buzza Cardzo, Anaheim, California, printed in Western Germany. Back of card with logo, sold for $1.00, 7.75" high, 9.5" wide, 3" deep, VG, *Kreider Collection*. $1-35

All three greeting cards with dimensional look, punch out cards in a series. Dutch girl, series 1260. School children, series #233, valentine cutout designs. Inside, this card reads: Dan Cupid, as Teacher your work will assign, to answer this question, Will U B mine? Little girl, series No. 425, valentine cutouts. 12 designs, all cards made in U.S.A., all sold for .15¢, all measure 3.5" high, 2.75" wide, .5" deep, EX, *Kreider Collection.* $1-25

Hallmark fold-out booklet, all three dimensional scenes, 1961, 9" high, 7.5" wide, NM, *Kreider Collection.* $1-35

Dirigible with two little girls and two
daschies, printed in Germany, 3.5" high,
1.5" deep, 2" wide, EX, *Kreider Collection.*
$5-50

Chapter IV
Cultural valentines:
Valentine's Day lore and customs around the world

The celebration of St. Valentine's Day can be traced to at least the 15th century and evidences of a valentine type celebration appear as far back as the third century AD. Even though romantics would like to believe in a fairy tale beginning for St. Valentine's Day, this just is not factual. The closest we can come to a fairy tale beginning to the tradition of exchanging amorous greetings comes from ancient mythology.

Cupid, the god of love, greatly admired Psyche, a maiden with the wings of a butterfly. She was the youngest of a King's three daughters. Cupid was so taken with her beauty that he fell in love. Every night he would visit her from a distance and dash off as soon as the break of day came. But her sisters convinced her that he was an ugly old monster, so one night while Cupid was sleeping, she took a closer look at him with a oil lamp and, to her astonishment, she saw that he was the most handsome of gods. In her excitement of joy and fear, a drop of hot oil fell from her lamp upon his shoulder. The burn awakened Cupid and he fled. Hence, he is usually shown with a cloth draped over his shoulder to hide his wound. Psyche was heart broken and searched for him from temple to temple. Finally, she came upon the palace of Venus and this is where all of her troubles began. Venus treated her as a slave and imposed upon her the cruelest of tasks. Cupid still loved Psyche from afar and would assist and comfort her without her knowing it. With Cupid's help, Psyche finally overcame the jealousy and hatred she felt for Venus and once this happened Psyche became immortal and was united with Cupid forever.

The most widely accepted version of the origin of Valentine's Day occurred during the third century, at the time when Claudius II was the Emperor of Rome. Claudius II did not take kindly to Christians and would constantly persecute them. There was a priest, *Valentinus,* who gave support to the Christians. One of his duties was to marry Christian men and women. The Emperor was very upset with Valentinus, for he believed that married men did not make good soldiers. When he found Valentinus, he immediately had him thrown in jail. During his time in jail, Valentinus became friends with the blind daughter of his jailor and eventually he restored her sight. On the eve of his death, February 13th, Valentinus wrote her a final note bidding her well and signed it *From your Valentine*, the first time those words were ever written.

Valentine's day is celebrated around the world. In Spain, Denmark, Germany, Italy, and France people enjoy the sweets and traditions that St. Valentine's Day brings. The United States, Canada and Great Britain are still the primary nations where the day has special significance. Valentine's Day is not a bank holiday or a business holiday, but prior to February 14th stationers and retailers promote it by selling anything and everything having to do with Valentine's Day for parties, dances and romance.

Black wash women, mechanical-flat, with easel back, artist signed bottom left hand corner of apron "Bonte," 6.75" high, 4.25" wide, NM, *Kreider Collection*. $15-225

People have a general fascination with the customs observed in other countries. In England there are many valentine traditions. For example, in Derbyshire, England, young ladies are awakened very early in the morning to look through their key holes and would hope to see two objects, any two objects. This would mean she would probably be married by the end of that year. If she only saw one object through her keyhole she had very little chance of finding her true love and being married by the end of that year. Another tradition relates that young ladies should circle a church twelve times and repeat these words, "I sow hempseed, hempseed I sow, he that loves me best, come after me now." Once this was accomplished, her forever love was to appear.

Irish lad giving his sweetheart a valentine, dimensional, 10.5" high, 7" wide, 2" deep, NM, *Kreider Collection.* $15-150

In various parts of Italy, a valentine feast is tradition. This comes from the ancient tradition of a Spring festival known as "Lupercalia" which was mainly for the young and concerned fertility rites. In Sicily, an unmarried lady would rise at the crack of dawn and stand by her window; the first man she saw would become her husband by the year's end.

In Denmark, a joking letter, or *Gaekkebrev*, was sent to a loved one. Similar to the puzzle valentines of the 1700 and 1800s, the man composes and sends a poem to his love but instead of signing his name, he makes a code with dots in which each dot represents a letter in his name. The following Easter (yes, Easter) he sends her an Easter egg and reveals his identity.

As you can see, there are many customs and traditions for St. Valentine's Day. The price for any of these cards can go quite high, depending on condition, size, age, manufacturer, artist signed, and **"The Heart."**

Oriental valentine with children giving oriental cards, no maker, made in U.S.A., 4" high, 3.5" wide, .5" deep, VG, *Kreider Collection.* $3-35

Bohemian type valentine, made in Germany, mechanical-flat, 8.5" high, 4" wide, EX, *Kreider Collection.* $5-50

Oriental valentine with children bearing gifts for St. Valentine's Day, flat, artist signed, Bertha Stewart, 5.5" high, 4.5" wide, EX, *Kreider Collection.* $5-125

96

Chinese children at play, flat, made in USA, no maker, 5.25" high, 5.5" wide, EX, *Kreider Collection*. $3-35

Oriental comic valentine, flat, braid still has original strand of yarn, made in U.S.A., 7.5" high, 6.5" wide, VG, *Kreider Collection*. $5-50

South American child bringing his heart to his valentine, flat, "Golden Bell Greeting Cards," made in USA, 5.5" high, 4.5" wide, EX, *Kreider Collection*. $5-50

Mexican boy waiting for his Senorita, dimensional, 6.7" high, 4.75" wide, 1" deep, EX, *Kreider Collection*. $3-35

Dutch boy in front of windmill, mechanical-flat, with easel back, artist bi-line, Ernest Nister, London, made by, E.P. Dutton & Co., New York, printed in Bavaria, #3847, 5.5" high, 2.5" wide, NM, *Kreider Collection*. $15-125

Danish walker, mechanical-flat, Germany, 4" high, 3" wide, EX, *Kreider Collection*. $5-40

Dutch windmill covered in blue forget-me-nots, dimensional, adorned with Victorian scrap turtle doves, HCPP and Dutch boy inside as center motif, cellophane is not original, 1930s, 11" high, 5" wide, 6" deep, VG, this card was originally a Jewish New Year card. *Kreider Collection*. $25-250

Scottish Lassie bringing an apron filled with daisies to her "Fond Love," dimensional, her skirt is made of HCPP, excellent example of the embossing process, 7.75" high, 4.75" wide, 2.75" deep, NM, *Kreider Collection*. $20-225

Scotsman with kilt, Art Deco style, flat, with original envelope, no maker, 4" high, 5" wide, NM, *Kreider Collection*. $2-20

Chapter V
Comic Valentines Through The Ages

As with fashion trends, so are there trends in the greeting cards business. Starting in the 1840s, the comic, "penny dreadful," or caricature valentine became popular and the popularity has continued until the present day. In the beginning, these cards were of a satirical nature, usually sent to someone you didn't like. They poke fun at someone's appearance, occupation, or personality. They also embraced social issues of the day, from intemperance to politics.

In the 1840s, two of the most popular makers of comic valentines, Thomas W. Strong and McLoughlin Bros., both from New York, imprinted there company names near the bottom of the valentine. The most popular form of printing the comic valentine was with a wood block, originally hand colored, but later the printing process was improved to include second and third printed colors. The comic valentine was sold originally .01¢ to .50¢ a piece.

By the early 1900s, the companies we are most familiar with today became a reality, including Hallmark, American Greetings, and Norcross. Then, just as today, the public was searching for a bargain. These companies gave the public a lot of card for their money. For the price of one of the old master's valentine cards, you now could buy dozens of cards.

Not only did the public want more for their money, but they also wanted to forget their troubles. The card companies knew then as they know now that people want to avoid unpleasantness. They are out of work, or worried about business, or watching the fluctuation of the stock market, or worried about how trade agreements will affect their lives. Imagine how the people felt during the War years and the Depression? You might ask, "how can anyone be thinking about love and marriage at a time like this?" Tackling this challenge and making a profit doing that is one of the major tasks of the greeting card industry today and yesterday. They watch the social and economical trends of our society and create cards in response to the issues at hand. They must carefully balance the right amount of laughter, optimism, and romance to create a perfect missive of love. For these reasons valentines are a reflection of our cultural history. Today you can find comic valentines from the early 1900s to the 1950s for as low as .50¢ or as high as $25.00 a card. Their value has not increased quite as rapidly as other types of valentine cards because there is a lack of interest in this category.

Caricature woman standing on scales, comic dimensional, printed in Germany, very unusual, 6.75" high, 3" wide, 1" deep, VG, *Kreider Collection*. $5-75

"Miss Neatum," flat, copperplate engraving, English, circa 1800, hand colored, 9" high, 7.25" wide, EX, *Rosin Collection*. $5-125

Comic character valentines, from Superman to Disney characters, keep increasing in value and today one of the hardest to find is a Gee Man card. Also hard to find today are original Betty Boop, Dick Tracy, and Little Lu Lu valentines. As time goes on and these cards are documented, the frequency with which these valentines appear in the marketplace can more precisely be known.

When buying old comic valentines, beware of valentine look-a-likes, such as Popeye, that were not the official cartoon valentine. There are popular knock-offs in the greeting card industry that were not properly sanctioned by their original designers. Today, these cards are also sought after, but their value is not as great as the original illustrator's design.

Within this chapter also are personality and movie valentines such as "Charlie Chaplin," "Gone With The Wind," and "The Wizard of Oz." Many collectors, from movie star fans and film buffs, seek everything they can find that relates to their particular field including ticket stubs or a valentine with a particular character on it. The movie industry is a powerful force that bears watching, from "Walt Disney" Studios to the "Power Rangers."

The Black Devil, flat, wood block, hand colored, published by *A. Parker*, 8.5" high, 7" wide, EX, *Rosin Collection*. $5-150

Black Devil, 8.5" high, 8" wide, EX, *Rosin Collection*. $5-125

There are many collectors who want others to think these categories are easy to come by. To keep the market price down, they quietly seek their favorites for the lowest prices possible, when in fact the favorites may be quite scarce. After you have collected a few thousand valentine cards and have only seen three Dick Tracy cards or two Lu Lu cards, what does that mean to you? Or how about the person who says to you, "You just can't find valentines to buy anymore!" Do not believe everything you hear and do not underestimate the pride and ego of the human race. These factors play a very important role in the world of a collector.

Druggist, original wood block, made in U.S.A, 1930s, 8" high, 7.5" wide, EX, *Kreider Collection.* $5-95

"Druggist," original colored wood block, same as previous valentine but colored, made in U.S.A., 8" high, 7.5" wide, NM, *Rosin Collection.* $5-125

Dapper Dan type valentine, colored wood block, the subject of this very early 1800s example of scathing humor is "dandyism," English, flat, 8.75" high, 6.5" wide, EX, *Rosin Collection.* $10-225

To A Wet, flat, comic, made by Rust Craft, Boston, USA, 1940s, 9" high, 7" wide, EX, *Kreider Collection*. $1-35

To A "Wet"

You weep and moan and sigh and groan
About "the good old days"—
Your recollections are "all wet"—
You mean the good old "daze"!

To A Stenographer

Not long will you remain unwed
You're fitted by vocation
To make a simply A-1 wife
And take a man's "dictation."

"To A Stenographer," flat, comic, made by Rust Craft, Boston, USA, 1940s, 9" high, 7" wide, EX, *Kreider Collection*. $1-35

"Railway Porter," occupational, flat, comic, wood block, 8.5" high, 6.5" wide, NM, *Rosin Collection*. This valentine can appeal to the comic collector, the black collector, occupational collector, and the railroad collector. $5-125

TO A RAILWAY PORTER.

"Big Bizness" valentine, flat, comic, attractive girl, 1932, made in U.S.A., 5" high, 6" wide, NM, *Kreider Collection*. $2-25

Big Nose valentine, flat, 8.5" high, 5.5" wide, made in U.S.A., EX, *Kreider Collection*. $5-35

BLUNDERING FIREMAN.

You are only a broken-winded calf, and spavined too at that.
It's great fun to see you run, with the grace of a Thomas Cat.
The only hose that such a bummer knows, is that which ladies wear.
And the only fire that you put down, is the rum you drink on a tear.
Some one the hose should turn on you, and drench you to the skin,
And try to wash away the bad effects of gin.

DON'T

Imagine that to Shine
in Football Is the Sole
End of Life.
Give Your Poor Brain
a Little Cultivation.
It Needs it
Sadly.

Occupational comic valentines, flat, 1930s, all made in USA, 9.5" high, 6" wide, EX, *Kreider Collection.* $1-35

BASEBALL PLAYER?

When we seek your batting average,
Way down the list we hunt;
The longest hit you ever made,
The scorer called a "bunt".

"So Be My Valentine" packet of 24 cards, printed in U.S.A., flapper girls on each card, original envelope with complete set of cards, five of the cards shown, 1930s, 5" high, 6.5" wide, NM, *Kreider Collection.* $10-100

Dopey, mechanical-flat, ©1938, W.D.Ent., made in U.S.A., 5" high, 3" wide, NM, *Kreider Collection.* $5-75

Donald Duck on inflatable duck raft, mechanical-flat, ©1939, W.D.P., made in U.S.A., 4.5" high, 2.75" wide, NM, *Kreider Collection.* $5-75

Donald Duck's Grandmother, 1962, flat, ©W.D.P., 3.5" high, 3.5" wide, EX, *Kreider Collection.* $5-40

Figaro, mechanical-flat, ©1939 W.D.P., made in U.S.A., 5" high, 3" wide, NM, *Kreider Collection.* $10-95

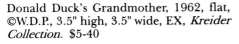

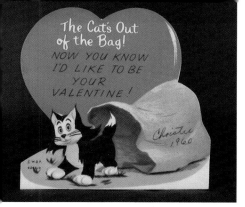

Figaro, 1962, flat, ©W.D.P., 3.5" high, 3.5" wide, EX, *Kreider Collection* Walt Disney's Figaro is rare. $5-40

Minnie Mouse, 1961, ©W.D.P., 4" high, 3" wide, Ex, *Kreider Collection.* $5-40

Wiley Fox, ©1939 W.D.P., made in U.S.A., mechanical-flat, 4.75" high, 3" wide, VG, *Kreider Collection.* $5-75

The Blue Fairy with Pinnochio, mechanical-flat, ©1939 W.D.P., made in U.S.A., 5" high, 4.75" wide, EX, *Kreider Collection.* $5-75

The Blue Fairy, mechanical-flat, ©1939 W.D.P., made in U.S.A., 5" high, 3" wide, EX, *Kreider Collection.* $5-75

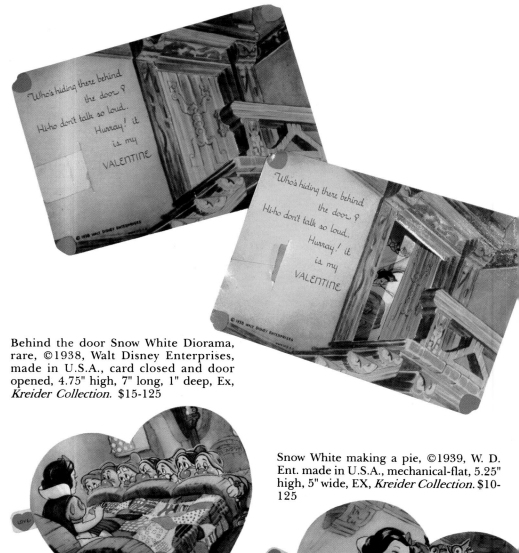

Behind the door Snow White Diorama, rare, ©1938, Walt Disney Enterprises, made in U.S.A., card closed and door opened, 4.75" high, 7" long, 1" deep, Ex, *Kreider Collection.* $15-125

Snow White making a pie, ©1939, W. D. Ent. made in U.S.A., mechanical-flat, 5.25" high, 5" wide, EX, *Kreider Collection.* $10-125

Snow White and The Seven Dwarfs, ©1938, W.D.Ent., made in U.S.A., mechanical-flat, 5.25" high, 5" wide, Ex, *Kreider Collection.* $10-125

"Gone With The Wind," reflective of the movie industry in 1938, flat, made in USA, 3.25" high, 2.75" wide, EX, *Kreider Collection.* $5-40

Popeye with axe, caricature, made in U.S.A., flat, 6" high, 5" wide, EX, *Kreider Collection.* $5-45

Little girl holding a valentine with a caricature of Popeye on it, flat, 1930s, 5" high, 3.5" wide, EX, *Kreider Collection.* $5-40

Olive Oyl with Popeye peering out from behind the olive jar, made in U.S.A., flat, 1930s, 6.5" high, 6" wide, EX, *Kreider Collection.* $5-75

Popeye, caricature, with Wimpy and Olive
Oyl inside, flat, card opens up, made in
U.S.A., notice Olive Oyl has blonde hair,
4" high, 4" wide, NM, *Kreider Collection.*
$5-50

Wimpy, flat, late 1930s, made in U.S.A.,
5.75" high, 4" wide, NM, *Kreider Collection.* $5-75

Henry, flat, made in U.S.A., 4" high, 4"
wide, Ex, *Kreider Collection.* $5-50

Jiggs, flat, made in U.S.A., 4" high, 4" wide, VG, *Kreider Collection.* $5-55

Shirley Temple caricature with a modern day Punch and Judy puppet show, mechanical-flat, c. 1940s, 6" high, 5" wide, EX, *Kreider Collection.* $5-55

"You're A Swinger," original Troll valentine, 1960s, U.S.A., no maker, 5" high, 4.75" wide, EX, *Kreider Collection.* $5-40

Charlie Chaplin image, flat, feet turn into easel back, 6" high, 4.5" wide, NM, *Kreider Collection.* $5-55

Hanna-Barber's Yogi Bear valentines in original box, 1965, sold for .59¢, Whitman Publishing Co., Racine, Wisconsin, box measures 9" high, 10" wide, MB, *Kreider Collection.* $10-125

Wilma Flintstone, 1962, flat, 4.75" high, 3" wide, no maker, EX, *Kreider Collection*. $5-40

Betty Rubble, 1962, flat, 4.75" high, 3" wide, no maker, Ex, *Kreider Collection*. $5-40

Pink Panther, all original Crush valentines, 12 per sheet, each measure, 5" high, 3.5" wide, M, *Kreider Collection*. $5-40/per sheet

Chapter VI
Nursery Rhymes and Fairy Tales

How old are nursery rhymes and fairy tales? No one really knows. Children and adults alike have been making them up for years and handing them down to the next generation. They take place everywhere, from villages and cities where they live or the woods where they used to play. A French poet, Charles Perrault, was the first person to actually write down and publish a series of fairy tales and nursery rhymes in the late 1600s. Most of them were stories handed down to him from earlier generations. These very early tales include *Puss n' Boots, Cinderella, Red Riding Hood, Sleeping Beauty*, and *Tale of My Mother Goose.*

Hundreds of years ago it was unwise to verbalize personal opinions regarding certain political and religious concepts. But through nursery rhymes, opinions could be expressed in a more acceptable form. "Mary, Mary, quite contrary" refers to the English Queen Mary Tudor who protested the Protestant faith. "Baa Baa, Black Sheep, have you any wool? Yes sir, Yes sir, three bags full, one for my Master and one for my Dame, but none for the little boy who lives down the lane." This is a political reference to unscrupulous trading in the wool business, where the Master and the Dame are the king and people in charge got the majority share of the profit, with nothing left over for the little person. "Little Jack Horner" was John Horner who was sent to London with a pie for the King. During that time important papers were sometimes concealed inside pies for safe transport (the streets were overrun with thieves). In this pie, deeds for several English estates were baked and greedy John Horner "stuck in his thumb and pulled out a plum," the king's plum, which represents the land deed for the Abbey of England. He stole the secret deeds. Another version of this story concerns English Queen Jane Seymour's brother Edward who received a pie in the 1500s from which some valuable papers had been stolen. The idea for the Little Jack Horner nursery rhyme, therefore, could date from the 16th century.

Grimm's Fairy Tales are a collection of German folklore. These tales were gathered together over the years, primarily by brothers Jakob and Wilhelm Grimm. They cared enough to want to write them down and share them with the world. They sat for hours listening to the stories German grandmothers told. Wilhelm made sure that every single word was written down just as the Grandmothers had told the tale to them. The first collection of *Grimm's Fairy Tales* was published in 1812 and it included "Hansel and Gretal" and "Rumpelstilskin," just to name a few.

By 1872, Hans Christian Andersen of Denmark finished his collection of fairy tales which include "The Ugly Duckling," "The Emperor's New Clothes," and "The Red Shoes." Andersen was honored by kings and princes, writers and artists. No one could tell a tale like Hans! He was the best! He himself once spoke about the field of fairy tales in these words: "To me, it represents all poetry, and he who masters it must be able to put into it tragedy, comedy, naive simplicity, irony and humor; at his service are the lyrical note, the childlike narrative and the language of nature description. In the folk tale it is always Simple Simon who is victorious in the end. Thus also the Innocence of Poetry...will reach farthest in the end." So the next time you read a rhyme or a tale to a child, remember they are representative of much more than just a happy ending.

Little Boy Blue, mechanical-flat, printed in U.S.A., early 1900s, Trademark G, possible series, 9" high, 8.5" wide, NM, *Kreider Collection* Back of card shows the trademark. $20-135

Little Boy Blue, flat with easel back, circa 1910s, 5.5" high, 3" wide, VG, *Kreider Collection.* $5-75

Little Bo Peep of the early 1940s, made in U.S.A., 5.25" high, 4.75" wide, EX, *Kreider Collection.* $5-45

Little Bo Peep valentine booklet, made in U.S.A., no maker, with original ribbon, and back of booklet, 6.5" high, 3.75" wide, EX, *Kreider Collection.* $5-55

Little Bo Peep, mechanical-flat, printed in
U.S.A., early 1900s, Trademark G, possible
series, 9" high, 8.5" wide, NM, *Kreider
Colletion.* $20-135

Little Jack Horner valentine booklet, made
in U.S.A, no maker, with original ribbon.
Also back of booklet, 6.5" high, 3.75" wide,
EX, *Kreider Collection.* $5-55

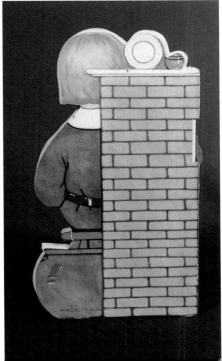

Little Jack Horner mechanical-flat, designed by Louis Katz, 1929, made in U.S.A., 6" high, 3.75" wide, EX, *Kreider Collection.* $5-60

Three Little Pigs, flat, folded into dimensions, made in USA, 4.5" high, 5" wide, EX, *Kreider Collection.* $5-75

Cinderella valentine booklet, made in U.S.A., no maker, with original ribbon. Also back of booklet, 6.5" high, 3.75" wide, VG, *Kreider Collection.* $5-55

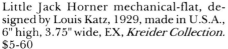

Three Little Pigs caricature, 5.25" high, 4.75" wide, no maker, EX, *Kreider Collection.* $5-25

The Big Bad Wolf, 5.25" high, 4.25" wide, VG, *Kreider Collection.* $5-45

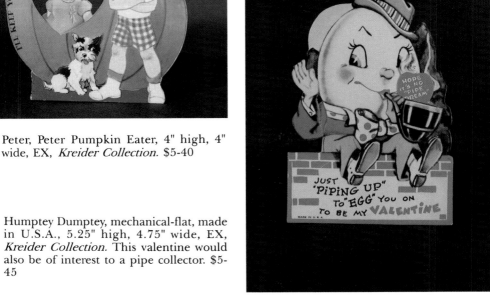

Peter, Peter Pumpkin Eater, 4" high, 4" wide, EX, *Kreider Collection.* $5-40

Humptey Dumptey, mechanical-flat, made in U.S.A., 5.25" high, 4.75" wide, EX, *Kreider Collection.* This valentine would also be of interest to a pipe collector. $5-45

Little old woman who lived in a shoe she had so many children she didn't know what to do, mechanical-flat, easel back, printed in U.S.A., 1925, unsigned but attibuted to Francis Brundage, Trademark G. Children popping out of shoe, 7" high, 7" wide, EX, *Kreider Collection.* $10-125

"Love's Life Buoy," Puss n' Boots type valentine, mechanical-flat, manufactured by *Raphael Tuck & Sons*, London, late 1800s, 9.5" high, 11" wide when opened, NM, *Rosin Collection.* $15-125

126

Chapter VII
Novelty Missives of Love

Novelty missives of love are probably the most fun category of valentines to collect. These are cards that have a playful or useful item attached to or incorporated into the card, such as a perfume container, puzzles, hair, handkerchiefs, or other item unique in style. This category runs from the 1700s to the present.

Plastics have played an important role in the greeting card industry, including valentines. Pyroxylin, invented in 1868, and Celluloid, invented in 1869, were different early plastics used in the greeting card industry. A fabulous example of the use of Pyroxylin is the banjo at the beginning of this chapter. In its original box, the Pyroxylin is hand painted and has discolored with age. The banjo dates from approximately 1910 and sold originally for $1.98. Celluloid appeared with many of the "choked to death" valentines of the "Golden Age" at the end of the nineteenth century. As the popular style for valentines moved away from delicate lacy cards, celluloid was one of the materials used to embellish the valentine, along with lots of ribbons, bows and knots. These valentines are important to include in collections and are increasing in value all the time. Celluloid was also used to make fans, business cards, religious cards, dance cards, collar boxes, dresser accessories, political buttons, picture frames, jewelry, clocks, toys, and all other holiday cards.

Imitation banknotes, checks, telegrams, drafts and postal orders are the most difficult to find today because The Bank of England and the post offices managed to have them barred. They looked too much like the real documents and some were actually made out by the "Bank of True Love". In America, imitation money was worded as valentines.

Another novelty are cobweb valentines. These date from about 1814 to the 1860s. The cobwebs were all hand cut, using the art form known as *papyrotamia*. The original purchase price was high, reflecting the intense labor of making these cards.

Also included in this chapter are a number of gift-giving valentines which include handkerchiefs, lollipops, or a stick of gum. Collectors of Irish linens and antique advertising certainly can find some marvelous specimens in this group to add to their collections.

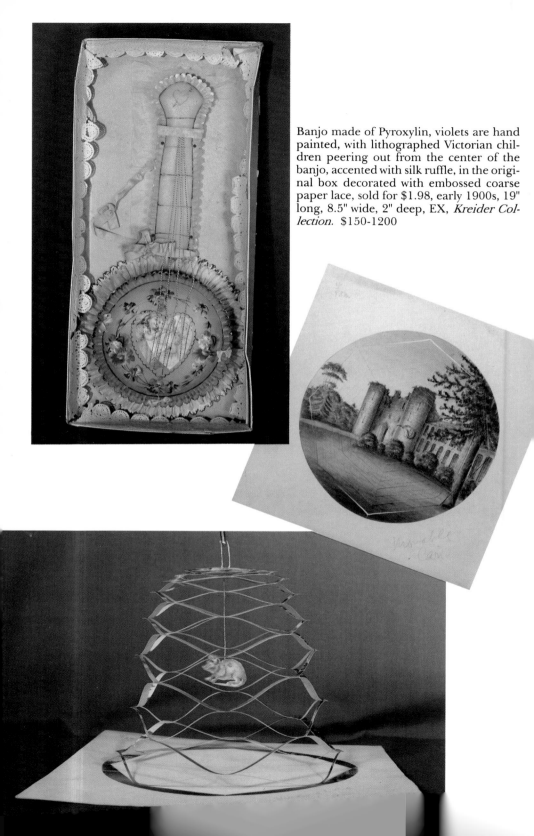

Banjo made of Pyroxylin, violets are hand painted, with lithographed Victorian children peering out from the center of the banjo, accented with silk ruffle, in the original box decorated with embossed coarse paper lace, sold for $1.98, early 1900s, 19" long, 8.5" wide, 2" deep, EX, *Kreider Collection.* $150-1200

Bank of Felicity, engraved lithograph,
dated 1883, 8" high, 4" wide, EX, *Rosin
Collection.* $100-800

Bank of True Love, bank note, engraved
lithograph, circa 1850s, made in the style
of an actual bank-note, these were so realistic that they were banned in England, 7"
high, 3" wide, EX, *Kreider Collection.*
$100-800

Bookmark, cameo-embossed paper,
marked *Wood,* English, circa 1840s-50s,
central medallion is beautifully hand
painted as are the delicate initials, 7" long,
2.5" wide, NM, *Rosin Collection.* $25-225

Opposite Page Bottom: Cobweb valentine,
lithographed on paper with embossed lace
borders, by *Burke,* English, 1840s, central
design of flowers evoke messages from "the
language of flowers," lifting cobweb's string
reveals a delicate hand drawn picture with
a message, 10" high, 8" wide, M, *Rosin Collection.* $100-1500

Valentine sachet, circa late 1800s, England, 4"high, 3" wide, EX, *Kreider Collection.* $20-150

Paper doll or undressed valentine, put together by hand, England, highly sought-after by collectors and difficult to find, 6" high, 5" wide, EX, *Kreider Collection.* $50-500

"Cupid's Token" poetry booklet, printed in Germany with original tassel, no maker, 5" high, 4" wide, NM, *Kreider Collection.* Note: the exquisite Victorian lady on the cover will attract people who collect images of particularly beautiful women of eras gone by. $5-55

Black cherub fan, chromolithographed, mechanical-flat, printed by *Raphael Tuck & Sons*, printed in Saxony, initial "H" printed at top of one panel, 10.75" high, 8.75" wide when opened, NM, *Barnes Collection*. This is a very unusual piece. $50-500

Folded heart opens into 8 different messages, original ribbon, hand colored. front of heart, heart when unfolded, and back of heart, 3.5" high, 3.5" wide, NM, *Rosin Collection*. $25-225

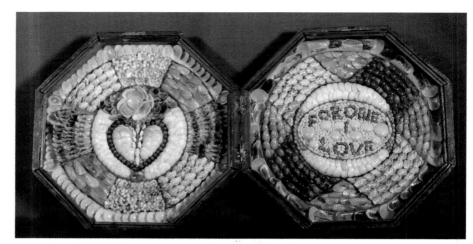

Sailor's valentine, a pair of hinged octago-
nal boxes, both with original glass and
frame, these were commercially made in
Barbados for the sailors, shell designs under glass show a heart, a rose, and "For the
One I Love," each section measures 9"
high and 9" wide, M, *Rosin Collection.*
$500-8000

"Oh Boy Gum," Art Deco artistry, with
original wrapper, artist signed but illegible
signature, bottom left "Rust Craft", Boston,
U.S.A., 4" high, 5" wide, NM, *Kreider Collection.* $20-125

Dutch Boy with original stick of Wrigley's Juicy Fruit Gum, 6.5" high, 3.5" wide, NM, *Kreider Collection.* $20-125

Here's a Valentine in LETTERS and Mathematics. 2. But it takes a stick of G·U·M 2-B- "sweet" enough = 4-U-

Gum card, manufactured by The Buzza Co., Craft Acres, Mpls. U.S.A., ©1926, Wrigley's Juicy Fruit chewing gum, 6" high, 4.5" wide, Ex, *Kreider Collection.* $20-125

I CHEWS YOU FIRST, YOU'RE MINE, BY GUM

Tute Fruite, with original gum wrapper, dated February 12, 1930, 6" high, 4.5" wide, EX, *Kreider Collection.* $20-125

"Cupid's Messinger," Bull Terrior holdin[g]
love note, flat with easel back, made i[n]
U.S.A., no maker, 9.75" high, 4.25 wid[e,]
NM, *Kreider Collection*. $5-75

Bull Terrier with message opened to rea[d]
verse, "Bow-wow, woof, woof, and a woo[f]
bow-wow, which means in dog language [I]
LOVE YOU!" *Kreider Collection*. $5-75

Bow-wow woof-woof
And a woof-bow too!
Which means in dog language
I LOVE YOU!
Edna Schmidt

"Love-O-Gram," Mickey Mouse caricature, illustration by Charles Twelvetrees, notice inital "C," 4.5" high, opens to 13", NM, Donated by Jack Wolf, *Kreider Collection.* $5-75

"Oh You Sweetness," with original envelope and original lump of sugar, Thompson-Smith Co., Fifth Ave., New York, 3" high, 4" wide, Ex, *Kreider Collection.* $5-75

Pekingese dog, mechancial, with squeak 'em toy inside and easel back, Germany, 6.25" high, 5" wide, VG, *Kreider Collection.* $5-75

Scuba diving valentine with original rubber hose attached, by The Fairfield Line, made in U.S.A., 8.5" high, 5.5" wide, *Kreider Collection.* $2-50

Young lady watering her garden with original rubber hose attached, 5.25" high, 8.5" wide, EX, *Kreider Collection.* $2-50

This darling puppy brings you this valentine heart-covered hankie in its original box, 8" high, 5.5" wide, 3.25" deep, NM, *Kreider Collection.* $2-55

Gift Giving valentine with original Irish linen hankie, chromolithograph with twins, surrounded by lilacs lovingly giving this hankie to you this Valentine's Day, with easel back, early 1900s, 8.5" high, 11" high, EX, *Kreider Collection.* Note: at first glance you think they are identical twins, can you find the seven differences? Answers at the bottom of the page. $15-150

*Answers: 1. eyes 2. bow 3. shoes 4. purse 5. hair 6. dress 7. hat

Valentine Paint Booklets, Carrington Co., Chicago, Ill, sold for .10¢, with original paint brush, paints, six valentines and instructions, complete set, 6.75" high, 5" wide, N, *Kreider Collection.* $1-55

All wooden telephone, all original, hand colored accents, easel back, copyright by International Art Publishing Co., 3" high, 5.5" wide, Ex, *Kreider Collection.* $2-95

Greeting card with original lock and key (inside), made by Barker, sold for .35¢, 6" high, 5" wide, EX, *Kreider Collection.* $1-25

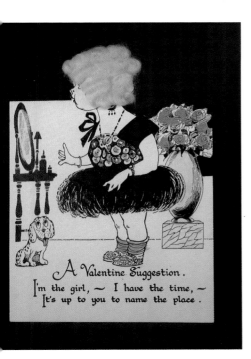 

Hand colored valentines, both embellished with synthetic hair, no maker, easel back, both 7" high, 5" wide, NM, *Kreider Collection.* $1-55

Loverville with original cast metal phone still attached, 4" high, 3.25" wide, EX, *Kreider Collection.* $1-125

"Heart Beat" clock work heart beats up and down once the heart is wound, No. 522, 1958, Fishlove & Co., made in Chicago, U.S.A, Kenosha, Wis., made for Coopers, 5.5" high 4" wide, NM, *Kreider Collection.* $5-75

Art Deco style gift giving valentine with original metal finger nail file, The P. F. Volland Co., Joilet, ILL, printed in U.S.A., 5.5" high, 4.5" wide, NM, *Kreider Collection.* $1-55

Clock work musical greeting card by Hall-mark, 1959, open up and it will play/turn key, sold for $5.00, 9.5" high, 7.5" wide, 1" deep, EX, *Kreider Collection.* $1-40

Original aluminum spoon attached, no maker, 1940s, 3.75" high, 4" wide, EX, *Kreider Collection.* $1-55

Original rubber band attached, 1938, 4.75" high, 5" wide, Donated by Betty Nickels from Stockton, California, *Kreider Collection.* $1-55

All original cast metal rake and violin, made in U.S.A., 5.5" high, 5.25" wide, EX, *Kreider Collection.* $1-55

141

Gift Giving valentine with original bottle of unopened "Sparkling Gold" toilet water still attached with original ribbon, Litho, U.S.A., The Fuller Brush Co., Hartford, Conn. 5" high, 2" wide, *Kreider Collection.* $5-125

Young man ready to give up his single life, 1940s, flat, with original thread, easel back, 10.75" high, 4.25" wide, EX, *Kreider Collection.* $1-40

Elephant dressed in red, white and blue playing the cymbals, mechanical-flat, with easel back, made in Germany, 7" high, 3.75" wide, *Kreider Collection.* $1-75

Button Boy with original button for his face, hand painted with easel back, 3.5" high, 3.5" wide, EX, *Kreider Collection.* $1-55

Ballerina with plastic eyes, mechanical- flat, printed in Germany, 8.5" high, 5" wide, *Kreider Collection* $1-95

Lollipop Gift Giving valentines all manufactured by Rosen Company, Providence,
RI, all came with a lollipop, late 1930s-early
1940s. These came in two sizes: 6" high, 5"
wide and 3.5" high, 3.25" wide. Color was
added and notice the size change: 4.75"
high, 3.75" wide, EX, *Kreider Collection*.
$1-30

Love Boat with original lollipop in plastic
sail boat, 5.5" high, 6" wide, 1.25" deep, M,
Kreider Collection It is very rare to find
this with the original lollipop. $1-75

Candy container given as a favor at a supper club, dated February 12, 1925, wonderful three dimensional affect under the lid, also bottom of candy container, has original manufacturer's label Laurent's since 1850, Phila., PA, .5" deep, 2" wide, and when open stands 3" high, EX, *Kreider Collection.* $1-65

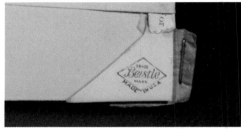

Wheel of Love, top and base made of HCPP, with mechanical wheel, 1920s, made by The Beistie Co., Shippensburg, PA, 9.5" high, 6.5" wide, 3" deep, EX, Donated by Mr. and Mrs. Richard Pardini, Stockton, California, *Kreider Collection* You "Wheel Watchers" out there would love to have this valentine! $1-95

HCPP basket full of hearts, dimensional, patents July 14,1925, and July 27, 1926, made in U.S.A., stands 8.5" high, 8" wide, VG, *Kreider Collection.* $1-95

From Dan Cupid, Florist, flat, embossed flowers with caricatures illustrated on them, 6" high, 5.25" wide, EX, *Kreider Collection* Does anyone really know who "Dan Cupid" is? $5-75

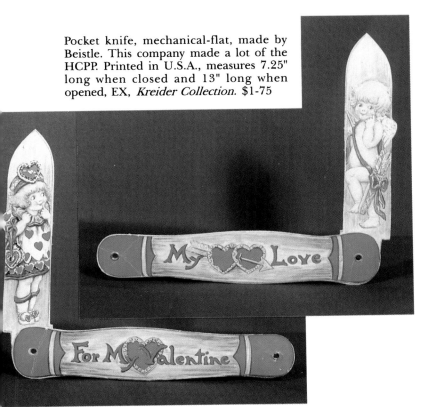

Pocket knife, mechanical-flat, made by Beistle. This company made a lot of the HCPP. Printed in U.S.A., measures 7.25" long when closed and 13" long when opened, EX, *Kreider Collection.* $1-75

Kalidoscope style die cut valentine with easel back, printed in Germany, 1927, 7" high, 4" wide, NM, *Kreider Collection.* $1-50

Dan Cupid's Greetings, Victorian child delivering a look-alike Whitney card inside the envelope she is carrying, flat, with easel back, 6" high, 3.25" wide, EX, *Kreider Collection.* $1-50

Chapter VIII
Topical Valentines:
Flats and Mechanical-Flats

Topical valentines comprise a major group among flat valentines from the mid-1800s to the present. They comprise the biggest area of spontaneous buying by the general public, aside from dedicated valentines collectors. There are so many subjects covered by topical valentines that people interested in special areas often find a valentine that fits right in with their interests.

Patriotic cards were a popular topic during the years of World Wars I and II. Many card companies advertised valentines for soldiers and civilians, as well as nurses during the weeks before St. Valentines Day, February 14th. Nevertheless, Valentine's Day card giving experienced a slight decline during the war years due to paper shortages. As with many businesses within the card industry, the decline was turned around once the wars were over.

Topical valentines most accurately present our societies' changes in fashion, occupation, and art style trends. The public was quite receptive to topical valentines.

Two influential art styles that changed the look of the cards were Art Nouveau and Art Deco designs. Nurtured in Paris during the 1890s, Art Nouveau's flowing, naturalistic style influenced many objects, from Tiffany glassware, furniture, lamps, bronzes, and jewelry, to automobiles and greeting cards. The Art Nouveau style, was characterized by curvilinear and asymmetrical design. In contrast, the Art Deco style, which emerged about 1925 in Paris, was prevalent in the greeting card world through the 1950s. The Art Deco form is a bold, yet streamlined and rectilinear form of design. This new design movement towards "Modernism" can be seen in the designs of public buildings such as movie theaters and railroad stations. The card industry portrayed these accurately on cards for every occasion and the public loved them.

Along with these style changes there came a new popularity for flat cards, like postcards, but in many different sizes. There were flat cards made to be sent to mothers, fathers, sisters, brothers, aunts, uncles, and just about anyone you could think of.

Unrequited Love, 17 known in the series, flat, wood engraved with an embossed border, Aquatint, mid-1800s, 9.75" high, 8" wide, M, *Rosin Collection.* $25-500

Man and woman courting, hand colored lithograph on embossed paper, circa 1940s-50s, 11" high, 9.75" wide, NM, *Rosin Collection.* $25-250

Sailor valentine, flat, wood block print, hand colored, octavo size, by *J. Wrigley,* English, circa 1825, single sheet, 7.5" high, 4.75" wide, NM, *Rosin Collection.* $25-250

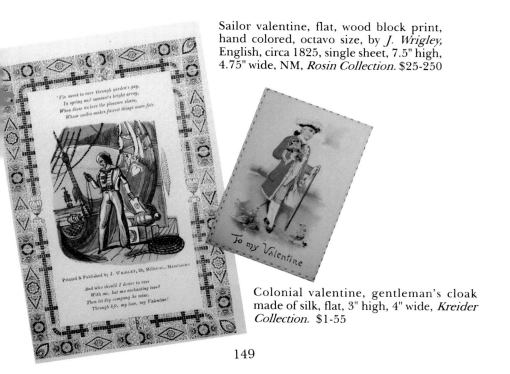

Colonial valentine, gentleman's cloak made of silk, flat, 3" high, 4" wide, *Kreider Collection.* $1-55

"A Gift of Love My Valentine," postcard-booklet, center motif is made of satin and violets are silk screened, booklet of postcard opened to reveal beautiful Victorian woman, design copyrighted by John Winsch, 1912, 5.5" high, 3.5" wide, NM, *Kreider Collection.* $1-75

"Be Mine Dear Love," greeting card, late 1800s, chromolithograph, unmarked, 6.25" high, 4.5" wide, EX, *Kreider Collection.* $1-45

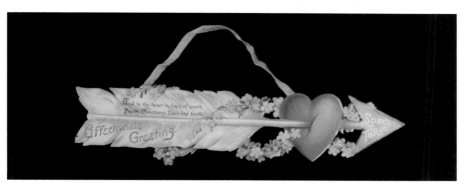

"Affectionate Greeting," an arrow through a heart, early 1900s, hanging-flat, embossed die cut with original ribbon, 2" high, 7.75" long, EX, *Kreider Collection.* $1-55

Heart, hanging-flat, embossed, chromolithograph border of pink forget-me-nots, Dutch boy and girl as principal motif, manufactured by Raphael Tuck & Sons, circa early 1900s, with manufacturer's logo, 8" high, 7" wide, NM, *Kreider Collection.* $10-225

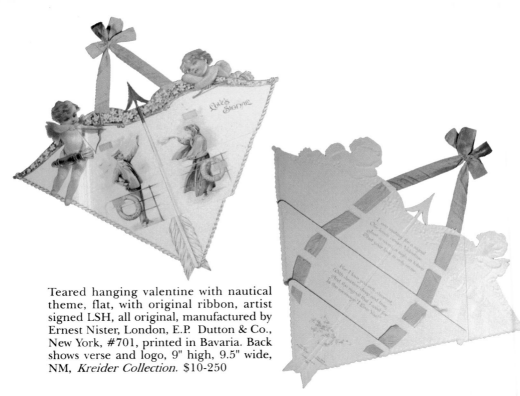

Teared hanging valentine with nautical theme, flat, with original ribbon, artist signed LSH, all original, manufactured by Ernest Nister, London, E.P. Dutton & Co., New York, #701, printed in Bavaria. Back shows verse and logo, 9" high, 9.5" wide, NM, *Kreider Collection*. $10-250

Victorian lady with muff, hanging, flat, ribbons not original, manufactured by E.P. Dutton, printed in Bavaria, artist byline Ernest Nister, early 1900s, 12.5" long, 6.5" wide, VG, *Kreider Collection*. $5-175

Cherubs in Hammocks, hanging-flat, five layer heart valentine with original ribbon manufactured by Raphael Tuck & Sons, early 1900s, 9" long, 5.5" wide, M, *Kreider Collection.* $10-200

Hot air balloon with Victorian children, hanging-flat, no maker, early 1900s, original ribbon, 9.5" long, 4" wide, NM, *Kreider Collection.* $15-175

Victorian ladies reading Sonnets of Love, adorned with pansies, forget-me-nots and clover that opens to reveal verse, chromolithograph die cut, easel back, early 1900s, initial "H" is on the back, 10" high when clover is opened, 6" width, EX, *Kreider Collection.* $5-150

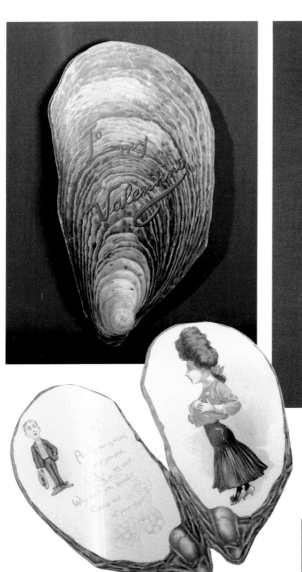

Fabulous oyster, chromolitho, flat, gre
ing card, designed by Raphael Tuck
Sons, unsigned, opened to reveal beau
fully illustrated image and verse. Ba
shows Tuck logo, 6.5" high, 3" wide,
wide when opened, NM, *Kreider Coll
tion.* $10-225

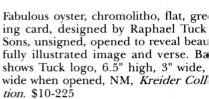

Precious child among the tulips, flat,
L. Prang, & Co., Boston, copyright 1883,
5" high, 4.5" wide, VG. While Louis Prang
is noted for his delicate artistary of flowers
and children, valentines designed by him
are very scrace. His cards sold for .60¢ per
dozen. *Kreider Collection.* $5-95

Sailboat with child holding Oriental lanterns, made with parchment and Victorian scrap, easel back, no maker, 12" high, 8.5" wide, EX, *Kreider Collection.* $10-250

Dogwood and darling children, flat, embossed, chromolithograph, accented with gold paper lace, late 1800s, 6.5" high, 6.5" wide, EX, *Kreider Collection.* $5-75

Cherry Ripe, chromolithographed, flat, designed by Walter Crane, published by Marcus Ward, London, it is from the book he did with Kate Greenaway in 1874, titled *Quiver of Love,* 9.25" high, 6" wide, NM, *Rosin Collection.* $100-500

Floral Arch, from the series "Children the Pond," 1876, chromolithorgraph card, designed by Kate Greenaway, print by Marcus Ward & Co., London, attach to lace paper and card folder, 7.25" hig 6" wide, NM, *Rosin Collection.* $100-50

I Found My Love Sleeping, from the series "Puck and Blossom," April 27, 1874 (reg.), chromolithographed card, designed by Kate Greenaway, printed by Marcus Ward, London, affixed to printed card stock with cherub motif, 7.25" high, 6" wide, NM, *Rosin Collection.* $100-500

156

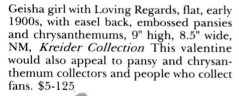

Geisha girl with Loving Regards, flat, early 1900s, with easel back, embossed pansies and chrysanthemums, 9" high, 8.5" wide, NM, *Kreider Collection* This valentine would also appeal to pansy and chrysanthemum collectors and people who collect fans. $5-125

Dutch boy holding arrow, flat, with easel back, artist signed M. Greinet, printed in Germany, published by The International Art Co., 7" high, 6" wide. Matching embossed postcard, series #829, 5.5" high, 3.5" wide., EX, *Kreider Collection*. $10-125

Love's Greetings, embossed, chromolithograph die cut, Germany, 16" high, 11" wide, VG, *Kreider Collection*. $30-325

Darling Victorian boy holding book, flat, chromolithograph, book open showing verse and bridal couple, easel back, 7.5" high, 2.75" wide, EX, *Kreider Collection.* $10-125

Darling little Victorian girl with origi ribbon in her hair, flat, easel back, design by Raphael Tuck & Sons, Series #1557, high, 2.5" wide, NM, *Kreider Collecti* $5-125

French bulldog with kitten, chromolit graph, flat, easel back, Germany, 4" hi 3.5" wide, EX, *Kreider Collection.* $1-3

Cupid selling hearts of all kinds, flat, easel back, 5.5" high, 3.5" wide, NM, *Kreider Collection.* Cupid's sign reads: "I am Cupid, a dealer in Hearts, Hearts all loving, and tender and true, hearts that stand firm and sure. Through the storm I am choosing a sweet Heart for you." $5-65

Victorian bust of lady advertising for a bachelor with original ribbon in her hat, manufactured by F. Volland & Co., Chicago, ILL, copyright 1914, easel back, 5" high, 3.5" wide, EX, *Kreider Collection.* $1-35

VALENTINE GREETINGS
WANTED SOON, a bachelor,
To woo me with devotion,
The work is light, the wages right,
With chances of promotion.

Unusual world valentine, opened to find "The Sweetest Girl in the World," designed by Raphael Tuck & Sons. This card shows the special artistry exhibited in Tuck's cards. Restored, 5.5" high, 5.5" wide, opens to 8" wide, VG, *Kreider Collection*. $5-125

Uncle Sam giving young lady a red heart out of his top hat, chromolithograph die cut, 3.5" high, 3" wide, EX, *Kreider Collection*. $1-25

Dutch maiden, flat, published by Raphael Tuck & Sons, unsigned but design attributed to Francis Brundage, 8" high, 5" wide, EX, *Kreider Collection*. $5-95

160

My Valentine heart, flat, unsigned but sign attributed to Francis Brundage, nted in Germany, 3.75" high, 4" wide, , *Kreider Collection.* $1-25

Little Dutch Maiden, flat with easel back, Bavaria, #1165, manufactured by E. P. Dutton & Co., New York, artist by-line, Ernest Nister, London, 5.5" high, 4.5" wide, EX, *Kreider Collection.* $1-75

d Cross nurse saluting the American g, manufactured by Thompson-Smith ., copyright 1918, Fifth Avenue, New rk, 5" high, 4" wide, NM, *Kreider Col-tion.* $1-75

onoplane, embossed, flat, ©H.L.W., with iginal ribbon, "H.L. Woehler," New rk, made in Germany, with easel back, 15, 3.25" high, 3.25" wide, NM, *Kreider ollection.* $5-125

Little girl giving candy stick to little boy, flat, Ernest Nister, London, printed in Boston, #443, 3" high, 3.25" wide, NM, *Kreider Collection.* $1-55

Cherub with pistol, flat, published by E.P. Dutton & Co., New York, artist by-line Ernest Nister, London, printed in Bavaria, #1819, EX, *Kreider Collection.* $5-50

Little Burglar out to steal your heart with a gun, flat, unmarked, 4.25" high, 3.25" wide, EX, *Kreider Colleection.* $1-25

Woman burglar with guns out to steal your heart, chromolithograph, die cut, 1920s, with easel back, made in Germany, 8.5" high, 4.75" wide, NM, *Kreider Collection.* $5-95

Unique big-eared golfing valentine, circa 1920s, with easel back, made in Germany, 8.5" high, 4.75" wide, NM, *Kreider Collection.* Possible series. $5-95

One cent wheat penny card, reflective of the time wheat pennies ran, made in U.S.A., 4.5" high, 5" wide, EX, *Kreider Collection.* $1-25

Senior citizen do'in the Jay, with original cotton beard, flat-stand-up, made in U.S.A., Campbell Art Co. Publishers, Elizabeth, J, designed by Ruth E Newton, 6.5" high, 3.5" wide, 2.5" deep, NM, *Kreider Collection.* $1-75

Cent valentine, flat, no maker, made in USA, 5.25" high, 5.5" wide, EX, *Kreider Collection.* $1-15

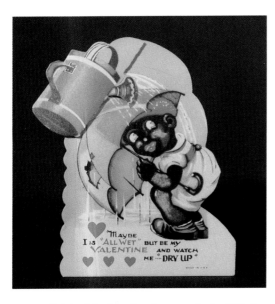

All Wet black valentine, made in U.S.A., 5.5" high, 3.5" wide, NM, *Kreider Collection*. $1-55

Valentine Police, flat, by Carrington Co., Chicago, IL, 7" high, 4.5" wide,, Ex, *Kreider Collection*. $1-50

Art Deco Lady with powder puff, flat, 1929, The Buzza Co. Craftacrer, made in the USA, 4" high, 5.75" wide, NM, *Kreider Collection.* $1-45

Four Whitney valentines, flat. As you begin to study the Whitneys, you will see that often-pensive little girls were used as the principal motif in many of his flats. All measure approximately 4" high, 3" wide or 3" high, 3" wide, EX, *Kreider Collection.* $1-15

Playing cards, flat, Art Deco style, Carrington Co., 3.75" high, 6.25" wide, NM, *Kreider Collection* This card would appeal to casino collectors. $1-45

Silouhette couple behind the curtains, flat, Art Deco style, made in USA, 7" high, 4.5" wide, EX, *Kreider Collection*. $1-45

Art Deco style couple at wishing well, flat, "Carrington Co.," made in USA, 9" high, 6" wide, EX, *Kreider Collection*. $1-50

Beach couple under umbrella, flat, Art Deco style, made in U.S.A., 7.5" high, 4.5" wide, EX, *Kreider Collection.* $1-45

Nudist Colony with child sticking its fanny out from behind a tree, Art Deco style, flat, 4" high, 4" wide, EX, *Kreider Collection* Along with black memorabilia collectors, this card would also appeal to nudist colony and Art Deco collectors. $1-125

Valentine Greetings For My Sister, flat. A Pastel Card, Doubl-Glo, 6" high, 5" wide, EX, *Kreider Collection.* $1-35

"Ah'm Still Waitin," Art Deco style, ar[t] signed bottom left hand corner L. Watso[n] The Buzza Co., made in U.S.A., 5.25" hi[gh] 4" wide, VG, *Kreider Collection.* $1-55

Art Deco lady with her puppy, flat, no maker, made in U.S.A., 5" high, 4.25" wide, EX, *Kreider Collection.* $1-25

Valentine's Greetings to My Mother, A[rt] Deco artistry, uncirculated, flat, silver fo[il] trim with original ribbon, Rust Craft, log[o] 6.5" high, 5.5" wide, M, *Kreider Collectio[n]* $1-25

Valentine Love To Mother, flat, with origi[?]nal ribbon, dated 1928, Rust Craft, Bos[?]ton, U.S.A., 6.5" high, 4"wide, NM, *Kreide[r] Collection.* $1-25

To My Valentine, flat, Art Deco artistry, 4" high, 5" wide, EX, *Kreider Collection.* $1-20

Art Deco boy on tricycle, 11" high, 5" wide, NM. $1-40

Valentine Greetings, flat, 1920s, Rust Craft, made in U.S.A., 6.5" high, 5" wide, EX, *Kreider Collection.* $1-30

Generic dogs with felt ears, flat with easel back made by Hallmark, ©Hall Bros., Inc., late 1940s, sold for .25¢. Both cards measure, 8.75" high, 6.5" wide, EX, *Kreider Collection.* $1-35

Teddy Bear, flat, accented with sparkles, made by Hallmark, ©1948 Hall Bros., with easel back, sold for .25¢, 8.5" high, 6.75" wide, EX, *Kreider Collection.* These last three cards represent the transitional period when Hall Bros. changed to Hallmark. $1-30

Plaid kitten for daughter by Hallmark, 8" high, 6.5" wide, EX, *Kreider Collection.* $1-20

Elephant, flat with easel back made by Norcross, New York, 11.75" high, 7.5" wide, *Kreider Collection.* $1-30

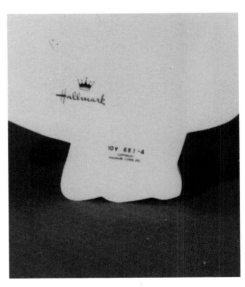

Dear Little Daughter, flat, greeting card with original ribbon, 1954, by Hallmark, came in different sizes. Back showing logo, 7.5" high, 6.5" wide, EX, *Kreider Collection.* $1-20

Stylish lady and Chesterfield cigarette pack, 5" high, 7" wide, EX, *Kreider Collection.* $1-50

Lady with Pekingese dog, 1940s, flat, with orignial pipe cleaner for dog's tail. $1-40

Walnut shape, circa 1940s, no maker, possible series, 3.5" high, 4" wide, *Kreider Collection.* $1-20

Sneaker, circa 1940s, no maker, possible series, 3.5" high, 4" wide, *Kreider Collection.* $1-20

Briefcase, circa 1940s, no maker, possible series, 3.5" high, 4" wide, *Kreider Collection.* $1-20

A Love Token valentine fan, held together by original ribbon, 14" when opened, back of fan with International Art Publishing Co. logo, New York, #7936. When closed measures 8.5" wide, EX, *Kreider Collection.* $35-350

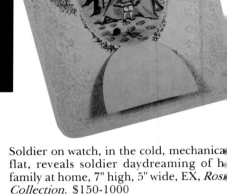

Sad and lonely solider boy longing for his love while having tea served to him by a waitress, 1922, mechanical-flat, Trademark G, printed in U.S.A, 9.5" high, 9.5" wide, EX, *Kreider Collection.* $5-75

Soldier on watch, in the cold, mechanical flat, reveals soldier daydreaming of h family at home, 7" high, 5" wide, EX, *Ros Collection.* $150-1000

Church in the Dell valentine, mechanica flat, hand colored lithograph, circa 1840 English, unmarked, quarto size, churc doors open up to reveal a wedding i progress, 9" high, 7" wide, EX, *Rosin Co lection.* $100-500

Civil War Tent, draped in American flag, mechanical-flat, shows tent flaps will open to reveal soldier writing a letter to his beloved at a "camp desk," motto "Love Protects," 7" high, 5" wide, EX, *Rosin Collection.* $150-1000

174

Sailor boy telling you that his ship has come in! Heart closed and with heart and eyes changed, Germany, 7" high, 3.5" wide, EX, *Kreider Collection.* $1-75

Paper doll sailor, mechanical-flat, no maker, 9.5" high, 3.5" wide, EX, *Kreider Collection.* $1-75

American flag valentine, mechanical-flat, with easel back, Germany, 5.25" high, 2" wide, EX, *Kreider Collection.* $1-45

Dapper Dan valentine with umbrella, mechanical-flat, embossed chromolithograph, die cut, early 1920s, printed in Germany, Trademark G, 11.5" high, 6.25" wide, EX, *Kreider Collection.* $30-300

Uncle Tom valentine, mechanical-flat, T-2, made in U.S.A., 4.75" high, 4" wide, NM, *Kreider Collection.* $1-50

Another Dapper Dan sitting on an ottoman, mechanical-flat, printed in Germany, with easel back, 7.75" high, 4.5" wide, VG, *Kreider Collection.* $1-55

Children allowing rooster to pick a valentine, mechanical-flat, manufactured by Louis Katz, NY, made in USA, 1925, with easel back, 12" high, 8" wide, EX, *Kreider Collection.* $5-150

I like diamonds and rubies red,
But I'd prefer a Valentine like you instead

Honey yo can't fool a Chicken Dey knows yo is my Valentine

To my Valentine!
You are an arrant little flirt; I like you, though you are so pert

Just gaze into these eyes of mine, And say you'll be my VALENTINE

Little girl flirting with fan, mechanical-flat, unsigned but design attributed to Brundage, printed in Germany, with easel back, 5.5" high, 3.5" wide, *Kreider Collection.* $5-65

"Yo'am ma Valentine," children in park, mechanical-flat, manufactured by Louis Katz, NY, made in USA, 1924, 6" high, 6" wide, NM, *Kreider Collection.* $5-125

Yo' am ma Valentine-Deed yo is Honey?

Generic dog and cat, mechanical-flat, early 1920s, G Trademark, printed in U.S.A., 8.25" high, 9" wide, EX, *Kreider Collection.* $1-55

Little boy with dog, mechanical-flat, early 1920s, G Trademark, printed in U.S.A., 8.25" high, 9" wide, EX, *Kreider Collection.* $1-55

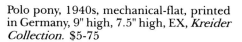

Bear cub coming out of stump, mechanical-flat, with easel back, Manufactured by Steiner Litho Co., Rocklin, NY, 8" high, 3.5" wide, EX, *Kreider Collection.* $1-45

Polo pony, 1940s, mechanical-flat, printed in Germany, 9" high, 7.5" high, EX, *Kreider Collection.* $5-75

Stockbroker, mechanical-flat, with easel back, made in Germany, 4.5" high, 3.5" wide, EX, *Kreider Collection.* $1-50

Monkey grinder, mechanical-flat, manufactured by Carrington Co., Chicago, Illinos, 7" high, 9" wide, Ex, *Kreider Collection.* $5-50

Movie director, mechanical-flat, with easel back, printed in Germany, reflective of the 1930s, 7.5" high, 4.5" wide, NM, *Kreider Collection.* $5-75

Pair of Dollie Dingle valentines with easel back made in USA, unsigned but design attributed to Grace Drayton, both 10" high, 5" wide, EX, *Kreider Collection.* $20-175/pair

Red lobster, mechanical-flat, initials H.B., made in Germany, 7" high, 5" wide, NM, *Kreider Collection.* $5-75

Little boy in yellow raincoat holding lantern to show the way to bring a valentine to his sweetheart, mechanical-flat, initials H.B., made in Germany, easel back, 6.75" high, 3" wide, VG, *Kreider Collection.* $2-55

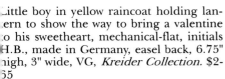

Girl with chestnut, mechanical-flat, embossed, chromolithograph die cut, initials H.B., made in Germany, 9.25" high, 6.5" wide, EX, *Kreider Collection.* $10-140

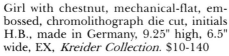

Bonnet Ladies, mechanical-flat, series, printed in Germany, 5" high, 4" wide, EX, *Kreider Collection.* $2-45

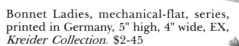

1940s ladies, mechanical-flat, made in U.S.A., 4" high, 4" wide, NM, *Kreider Collection.* $2-30

Wooden shoe sailboat with Dutch children, mechanical-flat, G trademark. This is one of my first three valentines my mother, Barbara Wolf, bought for me at an auction in Lampeter, Pennsylvania. $5-50

Heart flower, mechanical-flat, petals read: Open on St. Valentine's Day, with petals opened reveals a darling little girl waiting to be someone's valentine, with easel back, Trademark G, 5" high, 5" wide, NM, *Kreider Collection.* $5-75

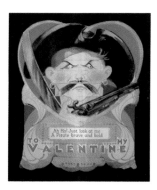

Airplane, mechanical-flat, goes up and down, 1930s, 6.75" high, 8.25" wide, EX, *Kreider Collection.* $2-45

Pirate, Senorita, Dapper Dan, all mechanical-flat, showing tab pushed up and pushed down, possible series, they approximately measure 4" high, 3.5" wide, all EX, *Kreider Collection.* $2-35

Ace of Hearts, mechanical-flat, with tab pulled to reveal the Queen of Hearts, printed in Germany, 7" high, 5.25" wide, EX, *Kreider Collection.* $5-50

Ace of Clubs, mechanical-flat, with tab pulled to reveal the Prince of Clubs, printed in Germany, 7" high, 5.25" wide, EX, *Kreider Collection.* $5-50

Goose, mechanical-flat, Germany, with neck fully extended through mechanical motion, 7.25" high, 2.5" wide, EX, *Kreider Collection.* $2-45

Ass, mechanical-flat, Germany, with neck fully extended, 7.25" high, 2.5" wide, EX, *Kreider Collection.* $5-75

Heart headed girl, mechanical-flat, made in Germany, 8" high, 3.5" wide, EX, Image 15, with eyes opened, *Kreider Collection.* $2-60

Scuba diver, mechanical-flat, pull tab and arms and legs move, no maker, made in Germany, 6.5" high, 5.5" wide, EX, *Kreider Collection.* $1-30

Dragonfly with cherub delivering his valentine greeting, mechanical-flat, Germany, 7" high, 5.75" wide, EX, *Kreider Collection.* $2-75

"To A Little Man" action card, tab moves the tiger's skates back and forth, 7.5" high, 6" wide, EX, *Kreider Collection.* $1-15

Big-eyed girl flying away on a mallard's back. Notice the interesting addition of the wristwatch to her arm. 7.5" high, 5.5" wide, VG, *Kreider Collection*. $5-65

English bulldog, mechanical-flat, big-eyed children on teeter totter, printed in Germany, 1927, 7.5" high, 12" wide (tab to tab), NM, *Kreider Collection*. $35-225

Big-eyed children in two-door roadster, mechanical-flat, with easel back, 1924. Notice girl is driving the car. Printed in Germany, 7.5" high, 9" wide, VG, *Kreider Collection*. $10-125

Chapter IX
Bits n' Pieces

You might be wondering where all of the handwritten verses on handmade valentines from the 1600s to the 1800s originated. There existed published Valentine Writers that proclaimed, "Don't write your own verses, we have something for everyone no matter what their situation." These published Writers were very inexpensive to buy, they sold for around 10¢. The earliest known writer in existence is from France dated 1669. English Writers were available in America by 1723 and both the British and Americans continued to publish these Writers through the mid-1800s.

Just as the Computer Revolution is taking over many jobs of today, the Industrial Revolution took over the handmade valentines of an era gone by, throwing the handmaking of valentines into a tail spin of woodcuts and engravings. The Industrial Revolution ran from 1840-1860s. The manufacturers tried to make a smooth transition from handmade valentines to manufactured valentines, by allowing space on the valentine to hand write and compose or copy a verse onto the card. Therefore, the "Valentine Writer" was still a major staple for the valentine card giver.

Salesman's sample book, Germany, purely for your enjoyment.

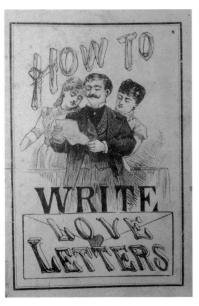

Valentine writer, rare, 7" high, 4" wide, EX, *Rosin Collection.* $125-500

'How To Write Love Letters..." this book is for the young and old, no matter what their condition in life may be, published by Frank Tously, New York, dated 1890, sold originally for 10¢, 6.5" high, 4" wide, EX, *Kreider Collection.* $15-150

Quizzical Valentine Writer, exceptional piece with insert still intact, 7" high, 4" wide, EX, *Rosin Collection.* $35-400

Little Flirt fan with the floral language of love, fold-out fan printed by A.J. Fisher, 98 Nassau Street, NY, 1871, 5" high, opens to 8", EX, *Rosin Collection.* $20-150

Valentines also were made as advertising pieces from the early years of the twentieth century. For example, Buster Brown was originated by Richard Outcault in 1909, and there are early valentine cards referring to the household cleanser, "Bon Ami."

Valentine cards for the blind are also available. Braille valentines go back as far as the late 1800s. These valentines are very difficult to find, but if you have the good fortune of finding such a card, it would do nothing but enhance your collection. Today, associations to aid the blind take new greeting cards and have them brailled for the blind community.

Loveland, Colorado, cachets and postmarks date back to 1947. In 1946, a cherub by the name of Ted Thompson, president of Loveland's Chamber of Commerce, and another cherub, then-Postmaster Elmer Ivers, decided to spread their town's love all over the world. They invited *Dan Cupid* to live in their town all year round, and the rest is history. In Loveland, Dan Cupid dons a pair of chaps and a 10-gallon cowboy hat along with his bow and arrows.

Mr. Robert Tholl, the coordinator of the *Re-mailing Valentine Program of Loveland*, reported that in 1995 over 300,000 valentines were mailed out from Loveland on February 14 with their famous postmark and cachets. With the help of the Chamber of Commerce and many volunteers, this program sends personal love notes out to 117 countries, on time, each year. The Chamber of Commerce holds a contest in the fall of each year to pick the winning poem that will be imprinted on the cachet the following year. In 1995, Elaine Beatty's winning verse reads:

A valentine is a treasure for joy,
To a heart that is loving and true.
A special sweetheart city cachet,
Is Loveland's gift to you!

A Special Greeting from Loveland, Colorado, 1995. Graphic design by Denise S. Erbes and Dan Looper. Verse inside by Denton L. Illingworth. Envelope with cachet. Design by Judy Sheets, cachet verse by Elaine Beatty. 6.75" high, 4.75" wide, M. *Courtesy of the Post Office of Loveland, Colorado, and Robert Tholl.* $1-5

Also in 1995, the graphic design of the greeting was by Denise S. Erbes and Dan Looper with the verse inside the card prepared by Denton L. Illingsworth and the cachet design was by Judy Sheets.

186

If you would like to participate in the Loveland valentine re-mailing program, you may enclose a pre-stamped, pre-addressed valentines in a larger 1st Class envelope and mail it to:

Postmaster, Attn: Valentines, Loveland, CO 80537

Your valentines will be removed from the outside envelope and hand stamped with the Loveland cachet, then cancelled at the Loveland Post Office. To ensure delivery by Valentine's Day, U.S. destined mail must be received by February 9th and foreign mail must be received by February 3rd at the Loveland Post Office.

Other towns also offering cachets for St. Valentine's Day are Lovejoy, Illinois; Valentine, Texas; Valentine, Nebraska; Loveville, Maryland; Loving, Texas; Loving, New Mexico; and Honey Dew, California.

Dedicated valentine collectors add at least one cachet and postmark every year to their collections.

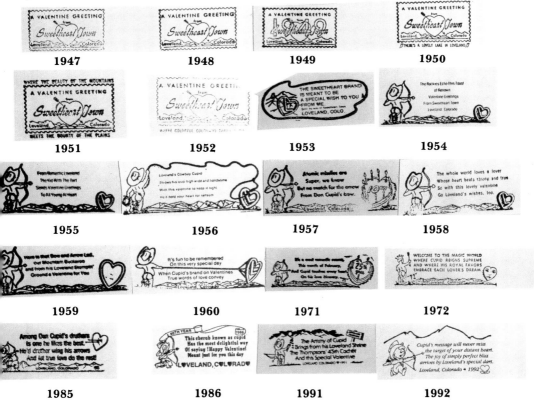

Cachets from Loveland, Colorado. *Courtesy of the Post Office of Loveland, Colorado and Robert Tholl.* 1940s, $1-20; 1950s, $1-15; 1960s, $1-10; 1970s $1-10; 1980s, $1-5.

Pre-20th Century English and American Manufacturers and Publishers

Rudolph Ackermann
Rudolph Ackermann, Jr.
Arthur Ackermann
Joseph Addenbrooke
American Valentine Co.
J. Andrews
Baldwin & Gleason
Caldwell Benbow & Son
Berlin & Jones
Bullard Art Pub. Co.
Edward Bollans & Co.
Bowles
T.H. Burke
Robert Canton
R. Carr
Catnach Press
A. Cortman Cox
Thomas De La Rue
Dean & Munday
De Marsan H.
H. Dobbs & Co.
Dobbs, Bailey & Co.
Dobbs, Kidd & Co.
Pasqual Donaldson
George Dunn
W.H. Elliott
Elton
John Evans

Abraham Fisher
Thomas Goode
Goode Bros.
Alfred Gray
H. Harwood
G.S. Haskins & Co.
Chalres P. Huestis
Esther Howland
S.A. Howland
G. Ingram
Jonathan King
Jonathan King, Jr.
George Kershaw & Son
Le Blond & Co.
Lloyd Bros.
Edward Lloyd
Charles Magnus
Joseph Mansell
Richard Marsh
Albert Marks
J.L. Marks
McLoughlin Bros.
George Meek
David Mossman
Mrs. Mossman
Mullord Bros.
N.E.V.CO.
Ernest Nister

Obpacher
A. Park
Louis Prang
J.V.Quick
Eugen Rimmel
Rock Bros.
H.A. Sanders
G. Smeeton
Thomas Stevens
T.W. Strong
George Snyder
Benjamin Sulman
T. Frere
Edward Taft
Jotham Taft
Torond
Raphael Tuck and So
Fred Turner
Marcus Ward & Co.
Westwood
Edward Whaites
John Windsor & Sons
J.T. Wood & Co.
James Wrigley

A Partial List of Manufacturers to be aware of from the 20th Century

Ambassador Cards
American Greeting Cards, Cleveland 2,
   Ohio and Los Angeles, 16, California
The Barker Co., Cincinnati, Ohio
The Beistle Co., Shippensburg, Pennsylvania
The Buzza Co., Anaheim, California
The Buzza Cardozo, Anaheim, California
The Buzza Co., Craft Acres Mpls., U.S.A.
Carrington Co., Chicago, Illinois
Campbell Art Co, Elizabeth, New Jersey
The Fairfield Line, made in U.S.A.
H. Fishlove & Co., Chicago, Illinois
Gibson, made in U.S.A.
Golden Bell Greeting Cards, U.S.A.
Hall Bros.

Hallmark, Kansas City, Missouri
Louis Katz, New York
Norcross, New York
A Novo Laugh
The Pastel Co., Double Glo, made in U.S.A
Rosen Company, Providence, Rhode Island
Rust Craft, Boston, Massachusets
Steiner Litho Co., Rocklin, New York
Thompson-Smith Co., Fifth Avenue, New Y
F. Volland Co, Chicago, Illinois
The P. F. Volland Co., Joilet, Illinois
Whitman Publishing Co., Racine, Wisconsi
Whitney, Worcester, Massachusets
H.L. Woehler, New York

The 10 most-asked questions when I lecture are:

1. Do I have to worry about reproductions?
Luckily, most of the reproductions are clearly marked. They will have the manufacturers logo and the year they were made imprinted on them. A time may come when this will change once the manufacturer decides to cut corners to save time and ink in the printing process.

2. Can I restore valentines and does this detract from the value?
Yes, you may restore them, but only use archival materials, tape, acid free backing. You need to be most careful of unscrupulous dealers who restore valentines and aren't truthful about it. Restoration is perfectly acceptable as long as it is done correctly, i.e. please make sure you match the same time frame on the card. You do not want a 1920s scrap with a 1940s scrap. With regard to restoration taking away from the value, once again that depends on my equation in the Introduction.

3. Are valentines more valuable with the manufacturer's logos on the back or embossed on the front of the card?
Again, the knowledge of the collector must grow before this becomes a definite standard. There are collectors who only collect valentines made by certain makers, like Raphael Tuck & Sons and so on. Ultimately, collecting valentines will be like toys, you will want the best manufacturer and mint and in the box.

4. Does it matter that a valentine has writing on the back?
At this point, no. Original old signatures add character to the valentine. Men who want to send an old valentine to a lady sometimes ask me if they should erase the old, original signature. I tell them, "No!" Just sign your name and put the current date on it. Historians of the future will love you for this! By erasing the signature, you aren't going to make the card increase in value. It has already been used, you can't make it into an uncirculated card by erasing signatures.

5. How can you date the cards?
There are four main ways to date cards: 1. By observing the fashions on the card. 2. By the manufacturer's logo that might be on it. 3. By knowing when a certain illustrator was working for a certain publishing company. 4. By finding out some history...Where the valentines came from? How long were they in the family? Did your Great Grandparents have these cards?

6. Where can I find valentines today?
You must look hard, but there are still plenty out there to find. Flea markets, antique shows, ephemera fairs, postcard shows, book fairs, or private collections. Ask every dealer you come in contact with, if they don't have valentines in their booth, they might have them at home or back in their shop. A lot of times you must bend down and look for them under the table and in baskets.

7. How can I store my collection of valentines?
Always use archival materials, not only for restoration, but for storage as well. **Acid-free** are the key words to remember. Keep your valentines out of direct sunlight, and for those of you living in the East, please watch the humidity! You should wear cotton gloves when handling your collection, which will keep the oils from your hands off of the cards. You can contact museums, art supply stores, or framing shops and they will be more than happy to guide you to the right materials.

8. What is foxing and can it be stopped?
Foxing is the discoloration of paper much like age spots on the human skin. Foxing is caused by chemical reactions and moisture, it can not be removed once it has started.

9. Buying valentines for love or profit?
I would never tell anyone to buy valentines for an investment. Buy them because you love them or you appreciate the lithography process. Granted, like any collectible, if you buy correctly, you probably will see a profit in time.

10. Can I have my collection appraised?
Yes, for a professional written appraisal for insurance purposes or just for resale purposes, contact a reputable dealer or appraiser.

Glossary

Acrostic: a verse where series of words of equal length are arranged to read the same horizontally or vertically.

Air Brushed: a fine spray of paint is applied to HCPP to give the card a varied shade affect.

Angel: one of an order of spiritual beings that are attendants and messengers of god.

Aquatint: a method of etching a printing plate so that the tones similar to watercolor washes can be reproduced.

Art Deco: art style of the 1920s and 1930s, expressed by using bold outlines, streamlined and rectilinear forms.

Art Nouveau: art style of the late 19th century, expressed by using waving and leafy type lines.

Artist Signed: the artist signs his or hers original piece of art work and the manufacturer then reproduces that art work, onto a card, resulting in an artist signed card.

By-Line: when the publisher gives the artist credit for his or hers illustration, by imprinting the artists name (in block style) by the name of the publisher on each card printed, (this is not the artists actual signature reproduced as with the artist signed cards that have the actual signature of the artist).

Cachet: a design or inscription on an envelope to commemorate a postal or philatelic event.

Calash: a light small wheeled four passenger carriage with a folding top.

Caricature: an exaggerated image that resembles another image; a look-a-like, but exaggerated features.

Celluloid: an artificial substance composed mostly of cellulose or vegetable fibrin. The compound is molded by heat and pressure to the desired shape. Used as a substitute for ivory, bone, coral etc.

Cherub: one of the second highest order of Angels, picture or statue of a child's head with wings.

Choked to Death: too much gooppety-goop-unattractive, too many ribbons, knots and bows.

Chromolithograph: a colored picture printed from a series of stones or plates.

Comic Valentine: a card that makes you laugh, a card not to be taken seriously, also may have character from a comic strip on it as seen in the newspaper.

Copperplate: a print made for this etched or engraved plate.

Cote: shelter or shed for small animals, birds, etc.

Cryptogram: a hidden message by using symbols or a code.

Cupid: god of Love, son of Jupiter and Venus, is represented as a winged boy.

Curator: a person in charge of an exhibit or museum.

Daguerreotype Valentine: a card with a photo produced on a silver or silver-coppered plate used as the center motif.

Devotional valentine: a valentine usually put together by hand, expressing ardent love or affection for someone or pertaining to the Bible.

Die Cut: the process of cutting paper into different shapes and designs, achieved by using a die.

Dimensional: measurement of length, width, height and depth, can have more than one or more layers to the subject.

Diorama: a scene that is revealed from a distance through an opening.

Dresden: city in Germany on the Elbe River, known for its manufacturing of gold and silver Victorian scraps and holiday decorations during the 19th century.(Saxony)

Easel Back: a support or upright made of cardboard attached to the back of the card.

Emboss: decorate with a design pattern etc., that is higher than the surface.

Ephemera: anything of printed matter that was meant to be thrown away within 24 hours. (There are several definitions of ephemera, but I find this one to be the purest definition.) It comes from the May fly that is born, breeds and dies in twenty-four hours. Examples of ephemera would be: George Washington's laundry list, ticket stubs, receipts etc.

Ethnic: large groups of people with common traits, customs, language, or social views.

Flat: smooth or level surface.

Fractur: a art form of penmanship giving each letter in the alphabet a distinctive appearance of long, sweeping broken letters with intricate embellishments.

Glassine: a thin, transparent paper, made of sulfite pulp, used in window envelopes, greeting cards etc.

Honey Comb Paper Puff: tissue paper made into an accordian type paper imitating a bees honeycomb.

Lithograph: picture, print etc., made from a flat, specially prepared stone or metal plate.

Love Token: anything given from the heart and soul of the giver. The gift could be finely crafted by the giver or purchased from a retail shop. Love Tokens could represent anything from porcelain pitchers to a walnut with initials craved into the shell.

Mechanical: anything with one or more moving parts.

Monochromatic: these are lithographs, usually in black.

Novelty: cards that have a playful or useful item attached or incorporated into the card such as: perfume, puzzles, hair, linen hankies; are unique in style.

Octavo size: the size of a piece of paper cut eight from a sheet.

Papyrotamia: the art form of making a cobweb valentine, which were hand cut into a continuous web.

Papyrotype: a photolithographic process in which the picture to be reproduced is first printed upon paper and then transferred to the stone or zinc.

Papyrine: a tough translucent imitation parchment, made by treating paper with a sulfuric acid path.

Psyche: means the soul, she is pictured as a maiden with the wings of a butterfly.

Pin Prick: a shallow hole or mark made with a pin or sharp instrument.

Pyroxylin: earliest form of celluloid, yellows with age, fairly light weight. (pre-celluloid) A soluble form of cellulose nitrate used in plastic compounds in the arts.

Quarto: Four valentines would be cut from one piece of paper resulting in the size of four 8" x 10" sheets.

Rebus: a riddle represented with pictures or syllables in sound.

Scherenschnitte: intricate paper cut work done by hand with a scissors resulting in one or more images to make a picture and then secured onto a contrasting piece of paper for a silhouetted effect.

Silhouette: an outline of a person or image cut out from a dark piece of paper, usually done in black, also can be hand drawn onto a piece of paper with ink

Theorem work: sketching an image onto a piece of oil paper, from there a stencil was cut out, water colors were then applied by using this stencil onto a piece of paper and would be finished by applying gum arabic with a brush to keep the water colors from running

Tin Type Photo or Ferrotype: a positive photograph made by a collodion process on a thin iron plate having a darkened surface, when this process is finished the photo then has a glossy appearance to it.

Uncirculated: never used, never opened, the equilvalent to mint and in the box.

Valentine: a greeting card or small gift sent on Valentine's day, February 14th; a sweetheart chosen on this day; Saint, Christian martyr of the third century.

Venus: the goddess of Beauty and Mother of Love. Sparrows and doves were used primarily to pull her chariot.

Victoria: a low four wheeled pleasure carriage for two with a calash top and a raised seat in front for the driver or an open passenger automobile with a calash top that usually extends over the rear seat only.

Victorian: pertaining to the reign of Queen Victoria, 1819-1901.

Victorian scrap: pieces of paper usually embossed and chromolithographed, resembling flowers, children, baskets, wreaths, trellises etc., used to embellished cards and ornaments, usually produced on sheets and then cut apart into individual pieces.

W.D.P.: Walt Disney Productions, was used after the 1930s.

W.D.Ent.: Walt Disney Enterprises, was used prior and during the 1930s.

Watermark: a marking in paper resulting from differences in thickness, produced by pressure of a projecting design in the mold, visible when the piece of paper is held to the light.

Woodcut: is the art form of carving an imagine into a plank or wood block and often printed by hand.

Wood Engraving: the wood engraving is cut into the end grain and the block is usually type high to fit into the press.

Bibliography

Books

Brindell, Dennis, *Valentine's Day*, Fradin

Carver, Sally S., *The American Postcard Guide to TUCK*, Carves Cards, Brookline, 1982

Etter, Roberta B., *Tokens Of Love*, Abbeville Press, New York, 1990

Hornung, Clarence P., *Treasury of American Design*, Volume Two, Harry N. Abrams, New York

Laver, James, *Victoriana*,

Lee, Ruth Webb, *The History of Valentines*, Batsford, 1952

Nicholson, Susan Brown, *The Encyclopedia of Antique Postcards* Wallace-Homestead, Radnor, 1994

Robacker, Earl F., *Arts of the Pennsylvania Dutch*,

Shelly, Donald A., *The Fraktur Writings or Illuminated Manuscripts of the Pennsylvania Germans* Pennsylvania German Folklore Society, 1960

Staff, Frank, The Valentine & Its Origin, Frederick A. Praeger, England, 1969

The Standard Dictionary of Facts, The Frontier Press Company, Buffalo, NY 1919

The World Book Encyclopedia, Field Enterprises Educational Corporation, Chicago, 1966

Articles

Baumgart, R.A., "Snip, Snip...Scherenschnitte," *Ideals Valentine*, 1979

Bird, Carol, "Louder and Funnier for Cupid in '31 Valentines," *San Francisco Chronicle*, February, 1931

Carroll, Judith T., "Valentine's Day, A Double Christmas for Some Post Offices," *Postmasters Gazette*, February, 1995

"Early Printed Valentines," *Spinning Wheel*, January-February, 1981

Emerson, Marion W., "Hearts and Darts," *Avocations*, February, 1938

Kreider, Katherine, "Valentines, An Era Gone By," *Collectors' Showcase*, February, 1991

_____, "Valentines, What To Look For," *Barrs Postcard News*, February, 1992

Wiersum, Beverly Rae, "From Loveland With Love," *Ideals Valentines*, 1979